JUDY BLUME

JUDY BLUME

A Biography

Kathleen Tracy

GREENWOOD BIOGRAPHIES

GREENWOOD PRESS
WESTPORT, CONNECTICUT • LONDON

Library of Congress Cataloging-in-Publication Data

Tracy, Kathleen.
   Judy Blume : a biography / Kathleen Tracy.
      p. cm. — (Greenwood biographies, ISSN 1540–4900)
   Includes bibliographical references and index.
   ISBN: 978–0–313–34272–1 (alk. paper)
  1. Blume, Judy.   2. Authors, American—20th century—Biography.
3. Children's stories—Authorship.   I. Title.
   PS3552.L843Z893   2008
   813'.54—dc22
   [B]   2007037491

British Library Cataloguing in Publication Data is available.

Library of Congress Catalog Card Number: 2007037491
ISBN-13: 978–0–313–34272–1
ISSN: 1540–4900

First published in 2008

Greenwood Press, 88 Post Road West, Westport, CT 06881
An imprint of Greenwood Publishing Group, Inc.
www.greenwood.com

Printed in the United States of America

The paper used in this book complies with the
Permanent Paper Standard issued by the National
Information Standards Organization (Z39.48–1984).

10 9 8 7 6 5 4 3 2 1

CONTENTS

CONTENTS

Photo essay follows page 66

SERIES FOREWORD

In response to high school and public library needs, Greenwood developed this distinguished series of full-length biographies specifically for student use. Prepared by field experts and professionals, these engaging biographies are tailored for high school students who need challenging yet accessible biographies. Ideal for secondary school assignments, the length, format, and subject areas are designed to meet educators' requirements and students' interests.

Greenwood offers an extensive selection of biographies spanning all curriculum-related subject areas including social studies, the sciences, literature and the arts, history, and politics, as well as popular culture, covering public figures and famous personalities from all time periods and backgrounds, both historic and contemporary, who have made an impact on American and/or world culture. Greenwood biographies are chosen based on comprehensive feedback from librarians and educators. Consideration is given to both curriculum relevance and inherent interest. The result is an intriguing mix of the well known and the unexpected, the saints and sinners from long-ago history and contemporary pop culture. Readers will find a wide array of subject choices, from fascinating crime figures like Al Capone to inspiring pioneers like Margaret Mead, from the greatest minds of our time like Stephen Hawking to the most amazing success stories of our day like J. K. Rowling.

While the emphasis is on fact, not glorification, the books are meant to be fun to read. Each volume provides in-depth information about the subject's life from birth through childhood, the teen years, and adulthood.

A thorough account relates family background and education, traces personal and professional influences, and explores struggles, accomplishments, and contributions. A timeline highlights the most significant life events against a historical perspective. Bibliographies supplement the reference value of each volume.

INTRODUCTION

AN UNLIKELY CRUSADER

Judy Blume never intended to be a political activist. All she wanted to do was tell honest stories that would both entertain and inform younger readers. So she created characters whom young people could relate to and who struggled through the same problems real kids did when growing up—loneliness, divorce, losing a parent, bullying, peer pressure, the body changes that came with adolescence, and exploring their sexuality—and as a result, her books became hugely popular, especially among tween and teen girls. Blume's ability to speak *to* her readers—not *down* to them—made her one of America's best-selling authors of young adult literature. It also made her books a regular target for censorship from religious groups and socially conservative political advocates. But it wasn't until a high-profile court case threatened another author that Blume emerged as a vocal free speech crusader.

> Congress shall make no law respecting an establishment of religion, or prohibiting the free exercise thereof; or abridging the freedom of speech, or of the press; or the right of the people peaceably to assemble, and to petition the government for a redress of grievances.[1]

The First Amendment of the Bill of Rights is meant to protect a complex array of rights such as the freedom of religion, a free press, the right to protest, and the right to associate with anyone you want regardless of their political views. In some instances, the First Amendment protects forms of expression that many people find disturbing. In *Virginia v. Black*, for example, the Supreme Court ruled a Ku Klux Klan member had the right to burn crosses as a political and personal statement.

Likewise, using an ethnic or racial slur may be vile and ignorant but it's also legally protected by the right that is the cornerstone of our democracy. That same freedom of speech guarantees everyone living in the United States the freedom to express themselves without government interference except in specific special cases.

Identifying those special cases, however, is a constant source of debate. Some seem obvious: While citizens have the right to complain about a president or disagree with government policy, they are not allowed to falsely yell "Fire!" in a crowded movie theater because it would recklessly put people in physical danger. But other instances, especially those involving personal morality, are far more subjective. Efforts to censor or restrict creative and artistic material and expression deemed to be obscene—defined as anything "patently offensive to community standards"—frequently leads to emotional confrontations between the opposing sides over what the limits of the First Amendment should be and whether a vocal minority should be allowed to dictate the standards for the majority. Television programs, movies, music, art, theater, and books have all been subject to censure in recent years. One of the most bitterly contested fights over a book's content took place in 2002–2003 when the school board of a small Arkansas town tried to restrict access to *Harry Potter*. The resulting court case attracted national attention and advocates from both sides of the issue were passionate in their response.

J. K. Rowling's *Harry Potter* novels have sold over a quarter *billion* copies, making it one of the most popular series in the history of publishing. Because of its widespread appeal, many libraries, including school libraries, stock the books so children who cannot afford to buy any of the *Potter* volumes can have access to them. A woman named Angie Haney did not think that was such a good thing.

In the autumn of 2001, Assembly of God Church pastor Mark Hodges gave a series of sermons about witchcraft and satanic cults—specifically aimed at the *Potter* books—that had a profound impact on Haney. She was raising two young children who attended school in Cedarville, Arkansas, a small town near the Oklahoma border. Haney worked as a deputy circuit clerk for Crawford County and like most parents was aware of *Harry Potter*. Because of Pastor Hodges' sermons, she was troubled that the *Potter* books dealt with magic and sorcery—even though she herself had never read any of the books to see if that concern was justified. But simply forbidding her own children from reading the books wasn't enough;

she decided *nobody's* child should have easy access to the books. Haney contacted Cedarville's school librarians, arguing that the books had little if any educational value. She also warned they could entice children to dabble in the occult and disrespect authority.

The school took her complaint seriously and organized a committee made up of fifteen teachers, principals, librarians, and parents to review the *Potter* books. The review disagreed with Haney's assertions and voted unanimously to keep the books in open circulation. According to established procedure, that should have been the end of the matter. But with the help of Pastor Hodges—who also happened to be a member of Cedarville's school district board—the morally outraged Haney prepared an official complaint and presented it to the district, saying the book

> keeps displaying disobedient behavior i.e. lieing (sic), sneaking out, fighting, name calling, it keeps reinforcing Harry doing all of these things with no consequences for his behavior.
>
> It demeans the parents. It demeans the teachers. This book teaches the kids to disobey teachers. Parents, teachers, rules are stupid or are something to be ignored. That magic will solve your problems. That there are "good witches" and "good magic." . . . It's a starting place to learn witchcraft, sorcery and other satanic ideas."[2]

In late June, 2002, the Cedarville School District board voted 3–2 to restrict access to all *Harry Potter* books, citing the potential danger they posed to impressionable children. School librarians were ordered to remove the books from open circulation. If a student wanted to read *Harry Potter*, they would need written permission from their parents.

Members of the original review committee were shocked and outraged. In an interview with the *Fort Smith Southwest Times Record*, Cedarville High School librarian Estella Roberts contended that the board's decision to restrict the series violated the Supreme Court's *Board of Education, Island Tree v. Pico* decision. In 1982, the Court ruled that students have a First Amendment right to information and ideas. Specifically, a school board could not remove books from a school library simply because the ideas they presented were considered unorthodox, whether it be about politics, religion, or other matters of opinion.

Restricting the books also made many parents very angry, including Billy Ray Counts, who had served with Roberts on the review committee. He and his wife Mary had a daughter named Dakota who was in fourth grade. They were just as passionate that she should have the freedom to read *Harry Potter* as Angie Haney was that the books were an immoral influence. So on behalf of their daughter, in July 2002, the Countses sued the school board in federal court, claiming Dakota's constitutional rights had been violated by requiring the state's permission to check out the book.

In essence, they claimed the books had been effectively banned. "The actual motivation of the school board was to limit children's access to literature that, in the school board's opinion, conflicts with its members' own personal religious views."[3] Billy and Mary Counts said they feared Dakota would be stigmatized if she were identified as someone who read books the district considered "evil . . . Children carrying the book with them in the school will be known to be carrying the bad book."[4] In addition, the suit claimed the board's decision undermined the school library committee's rights to determine the suitability of material.

Put on the defensive, the board maintained they had not banned the book but had merely taken away access from children unless there was parental permission. But the Counts' attorney, Brian Meadors, argued that the heart of the issue was free speech; J. K. Rowling had the right to tell stories about wizards without having to worry about her books being taken off library shelves.

"In this case, they have taken a particular (type) of speech . . . and treated it differently," Meadors told the *Times Record*. "Heavy-handed bureaucrats on the Cedarville School Board are trying to use government as a tool for censorship and to impose their own peculiar religious views . . . It's not like the books are in a gray area," he added. "They are the most innocuous books you'll ever want to see; they're totally wholesome books. I don't understand it."[5]

This wasn't the first time Rowling's book had incurred the wrath of fundamentalist Christian religious leaders. All around the country Rowling found herself in the eye of a censorship storm. In November 2000, the Santa Fe Independent School District imposed restrictions on the use of *Harry Potter*, requiring parental permission. In March the following year, a religious leader held a book burning that included *Harry Potter* and other books deemed offensive.

In November 2001, a Lewiston, Maine, group calling themselves The Jesus Party publicly condemned Rowling and shredded one of the *Harry Potter* books with scissors. Students attending the Agassiz Middle School in Fargo, North Dakota, had a field trip to see the first *Harry Potter* film canceled after a few parents—and a local radio show host—complained the movie was about witchcraft. Alamagordo, New Mexico, was the site of another public book burning in December of 2001, by parishioners from the Christ Community Church. The group's leader, Jack Brock, admitted he had never read any of the books but maintained they seduced children to the dark side.

FIGHTING BACK

Haney's action against Rowling's books was just the latest after years of bannings, burnings, and censorship. So the Cedarville court case represented much more than a disagreement between parents and school board members. Freedom of speech itself was on trial and many authors believed they were in direct danger of having their creativity and ideas silenced if the Cedarville School Board won—none more so than Judy Blume.

In March, 2003, Blume and others submitted a brief, or statement, in federal court supporting the Counts' efforts to overturn the Cedarville School Board's decision restricting the book and requiring written parental permission. Even though Blume and the other organizations were not the ones suing the Cedarville School Board, nonparticipants are allowed to file *amicus curiae*—a Latin phrase meaning "friend of the court"—briefs, if the court's decision may have a direct impact on their own personal interests.

Besides Blume, the plaintiffs named in the suit included American Booksellers Foundation for Free Expression, Americans United for Separation of Church and State, the Association of American Publishers, the Association of Booksellers for Children, the Center for First Amendment Rights, the Children's Book Council, Feminists for Free Expression, the Freedom to Read Foundation, the National Coalition Against Censorship, Peacefire, PEN American Center, People for the American Way Foundation, Student Press Law Center, and Washington Area Lawyers for the Arts. It marked the first time free speech advocates waged a legal challenge to library restrictions imposed by public schools.

According to the amicus brief, "The board's decision to censor these excellent books tramples on the students' fundamental right to receive information and ideas . . . and the removal of the books from the open library shelves violates the First Amendment to the Constitution, impermissibly restricting students' ability to explore, to learn and to enjoy."[6]

Chris Finan, president of the American Booksellers Foundation for Free Expression (ABFFE), accused the Cedarville School District of "stigmatizing this material for people who don't know who Harry Potter is. People say, *What's the big deal about asking for parental permission?* But if a book is not on the shelves, then a child cannot find it. If the child goes to the parent for permission and the parent doesn't know about the book, the parent might think there is a good reason [for the restriction] and say *No*. It makes it less likely for kids to get access to it. That is a serious First Amendment issue."[7]

It's important to remember that the attacks on Rowling, Blume, and other authors came from a very small but very vocal and very organized minority. The majority of mainstream religious organizations found the Potter books imaginative and positive. *Christianity Today* magazine called the book series, "a *Book of Virtues* with a pre-adolescent funny bone. Amid the laugh-out-loud scenes are wonderful examples of compassion, loyalty, courage, friendship, and even self-sacrifice."[8]

Blume had come to Rowling's defense before. In a first-person article published by the *New York Times* on October 22, 1999, Blume observed that the attacks on *Harry Potter* reflected a growing move toward censorship—by *both* sides of the political spectrum. She also said she knew *Harry Potter* was going to be a target.

"The only surprise is that it took so long—as long as it took for the zealots who claim they're protecting children from evil . . . to discover that children actually like these books.

"In my books, it's reality that's seen as corrupting. With Harry Potter, the perceived danger is fantasy. The real danger is not in the books, but in laughing off those who would ban them. . . . What began with the religious right has spread to the politically correct,"[9] she noted, recalling the uproar that occurred in Brooklyn in 1998 when a teacher was criticized for reading a book entitled *Nappy Hair* to her class.

Blume believed that the situation had gotten so extreme that "some parents believe they have the right to demand immediate removal of any book for any reason from school or classroom libraries."[10]

Instead of a jury trial, the case took place in a U.S. Federal District Court and was overseen by Judge Jimm Hendren. Both sides presented written and oral arguments. Attorney Brian Meadors was particularly disturbed because any child who submitted signed permission slips would, by the school's own admission, be placed on a special list. "Under the new restrictions, Dakota can no longer view the Harry Potter books anonymously. The Cedarville policy has the effect of stigmatizing or singling out students who want to view Harry Potter books."[11]

Dave Hogue, representing the Cedarville School District, dismissed Meadors's concerns, telling the court: "An 'injury in fact' is required to be shown to give rise to a case or controversy under the Constitution. This is not present in this case."[12]

The judge disagreed. On April 22, 2003, Judge Hendren issued a nineteen-page decision, ordering the Cedarville School District to make the *Potter* books available for general circulation in its school libraries "where they can be accessed without any restrictions other than those administrative restrictions that apply to all works of fiction in the libraries of the district."[13]

Hendren noted that recent Supreme Court decisions "stress the importance of freedom of speech in the education of America's youth" and recognize "that a school library is an environment especially appropriate for the recognition of the First Amendment rights of students. . . . The stigmatizing effect of having to have parental permission to check out a book constitutes a restriction on access."[14]

The judge also ruled that school board members had improperly restricted access to the books "because of their shared belief that the books promote a particular religion. Regardless of the personal distaste with which these individuals regard 'witchcraft,' it is not properly within their power and authority as members of defendant's school board to prevent the students at Cedarville from reading about it."[15]

The order was effective immediately.

Free speech proponents hailed the ruling as a landmark decision. "This court has rescued Harry Potter from the clutches of religious hysteria," said Barry W. Lynn, Americans United executive director. "Instead of waving a magic wand, the judge waved the Constitution. In America, that's more than enough."[16]

A spokesman for Scholastic Inc. said in an official statement, "We're proud to publish the Harry Potter books. We think they're about good and evil and we don't believe in censorship."[17]

"The good guys won," a jubilant Brian Meadors told reporters. "We went to the federal courts seeking justice and the court gave us that release. We're very happy about that. Everybody is just thrilled with the decision."[18]

Well, not everyone. When contacted, the Cedarville School District had no comment.

It was a resounding victory for free speech advocates in general and school children in particular. But it was just one battle in an ongoing war; a conflict that Blume—mother, wife, grandmother, award-winning author—has been front and center of for decades. Her private life has been equally as dramatic and challenging as the plot of a book. Although Judy Blume only wanted to be a storyteller, her commitment to readers, her refusal to compromise her ideals, her dedication to writing honestly and with respect for the intelligence of her audience, have made her an enduring role model and icon for adolescents, past, present, and future.

NOTES

1. The United States Constitution Online, http://www.usconstitution.net/const.html.

2. John T. Anderson, *The Times Record*, April 23, 2003, http://swtimes.com/articles/2003/04/23/news/export63254.txt.

3. *Counts v. Cedarville School District*, No. 02–2155 (W.D.Ark. April 22, 2003).

4. Ibid.

5. John T. Anderson, *The Times Record*, April 27, 2003, http://swtimes.com/articles/2003/04/27/insight/export63388.txt.

6. Center for Individual Freedom, *What Do Harry Potter, Captain Underpants and Huck Finn Have in Common?* http://www.cfif.org/htdocs/legal_issues/legal_updates/first_amendment_cases/harry_potter_censorship.htm (accessed July 13, 2007).

7. "Put Harry Potter Back on Shelves, Group Asks," AP Press Release, March 4, 2003.

8. "Why We Like Harry Potter: The Series Is a *Book of Virtues* With a Pre-adolescent Funny Bone," editorial, *Christianity Today*, January 10, 2000, http://www.ctlibrary.com/2577 (accessed July 13, 2007).

9. Judy Blume, "Is Harry Potter Evil?" *New York Times*, October 22, 1999, http://select.nytimes.com/search/restricted/article?res=F70A12FA3A5D0C718EDDA90994D1494D81.

10. Ibid.

11. *Counts v. Cedarville School District*, No. 02–2155 (W.D.Ark. April 22, 2003) documents.

12. Ibid.

13. *Counts v. Cedarville School District* Decision, www.arwd.uscourts.gov/go/files/02–2155-mo-wp (accessed July 13, 2007).

14. Ibid.

15. Ibid.

16. "Federal Court Foils Arkansas School's Effort to Restrict Harry Potter," *Church & State*, June 2003, http://findarticles.com/p/articles/mi_qa3944/is_200306/ai_n9283016.

17. Caryn Rousseau, "Judge Orders Harry Potter Back Onto Shelves," *Associated Press*, April 22, 2003.

18. John T. Anderson, *The Times Record*, April 25, 2003, http://swtimes.com/articles/2003/04/25/news/export63334.txt.

Chapter 1

A VIVID CHILDHOOD

On average, our earliest memories go back to when we were three to three and a half years old. For most people, they are just vague impressions, like out-of-focus images. Not for Judy Blume. Her memories of childhood are uniquely and vividly imprinted in her mind's eye. While she might not be able to tell you where she left her car keys, she remembers how things felt, even "how they smelled. A lot of people put their childhoods away. I never did," so it's easy for Judy to project herself back "to certain stages in my life." And she writes about "what I know is true of kids going through those same stages."[1]

That ability to conjure not just the events but the emotions of youth is one reason her books resonate so deeply with young readers. However, as a little girl growing up in Elizabeth, New Jersey—a blue-collar, predominantly Catholic community—Judy had no idea her experiences would one day help other kids better navigate through the complicated, confusing, and sometimes unnerving years of adolescence.

Judith Sussman was born February 12, 1938. Her mom Esther was a homemaker and her dad Rudolph was a dentist. Her parents had both been born and raised in Elizabeth and began dating when they were teenagers. They got married after Rudolph graduated from medical school and started his dental practice. Judy has one sibling, David, who is four years older.

Judy developed an interest in boys early. She laughs that when she was just six, she was in love with *two* boys: Jimmy and Tommy. Amazingly, she's still in touch with Jimmy, who runs a prestigious dental school.

Judy says her family was a lot like the one depicted in *Starring Sally J. Freedman As Herself,* her most autobiographical book. She says, "Mother was [the type who would say], *No, no, don't, you'll hurt yourself, that's dangerous.*"[2] Her dad, who was Judy's hero, enjoyed talking to people and his patients often sought out his advice about personal problems. But Judy was never able to do that. She thinks it's harder for a child to talk to a parent than other people because, "You have to see him again in the morning."[3]

Even if she wasn't comfortable confiding in him, Judy was extremely close to her father and enjoyed spending time with him while he built things in his basement workshop. "When I was small he would sit me up on the workbench, with a hammer and nails so that I would feel included and sharing something special with him."[4]

Judy describes herself as a shy, skinny, child of suburbia who suffered from eczema. "I enjoyed drama, dancing, singing, painting and performing. I loved to roller skate. I also loved going to the movies, browsing at the public library,"[5] and looking at the bones of her feet in X-ray machines. Judy also loved dolls and says she played with them "in very dark and mysterious ways."[6]

She would also play in a dark and mysterious place. One of her favorite hideouts was the attic, where she would play dress-up, act out stories, and make up adventures while playing with her dolls. Although she spent a lot of time alone as a younger child, her imagination kept her from being lonely. "I was a great daydreamer. You know what I worry about? I worry that kids today don't have enough time to just sit and daydream. I was a great pretender, always making up stories inside my head. Stories and stories and stories.[7]

"I made up stories while I bounced a ball against the side of our house," she recalls. "I made up stories playing with paper dolls. And I made them up while I practiced the piano, by pretending to give piano lessons. I even kept a notebook with the names of my pretend students and how they were doing. . . . I was inventing, always. But I never wrote down any of my stories. And I never told anyone about them."[8]

Judy regularly fantasized about what she would be when she grew up. "I dreamed about becoming a cowgirl, a detective, a spy, a great actress, or a ballerina," because they seemed to live exciting lives. She had no interest in being "a dentist, like my father, or a homemaker, like my mother—and certainly not a writer, although I always loved to read. I didn't know anything about writers. It never occurred to me they were regular people and that I could grow up to become one."[9]

The downside of having an incredibly active imagination was that Judy was fearful as a child—of the dark, the basement, and even thunder. She recalls that her older brother "delighted in torturing me; taking advantage of my fears, jumping out of the shadows with a sheet over his head while making ghostly sounds."[10]

She remembers that even everyday activities could fill her with dread, such as walking to and from Victor Mravlag Elementary School, which was only two blocks away from her home. "The walk to school was an adventure because when I was very young I was afraid of dogs. On most days my friend, Barry, and I walked together. He helped me feel more secure."[11]

Even after she stopped being afraid of dogs, Judy didn't have much luck with them as pets. Her brother wanted a dog, so their dad brought home and black and white puppy named Skippy. But he ran away—or was stolen—and never returned home. The next family dog was a brown mutt they named Teddy. In the car on the way home from getting Teddy, he was very affectionate to Judy, but threw up on her. They discovered that Teddy threw up every time he went for a car ride. They ended up giving Teddy back.

One day Judy's dad announced they were going to take a ride in the Goodyear blimp. Even though she was afraid, Judy went, explaining, "Adventure beckoned." The experience eased some of her innate anxiety. So did the two winters she spent in Florida with her mother and brother. When she was in third grade, Judy's brother David developed a serious kidney infection. So in 1947, while Rudolph stayed behind in Elizabeth running his dental practice, Esther relocated to Miami Beach, Florida, with David and Judy in hopes the balmy, tropical climate would improve his health.

Initially, Judy was unhappy in Miami Beach. She was homesick for her dad and she didn't know anybody. But within a few weeks Judy had started making friends and she now remembers Florida as being a wonderful adventure, calling those two years "the most memorable years of my childhood." The family rented "a tiny apartment in a pink stucco building with a goldfish pond in the courtyard. My brother and I slept on day-beds in the living room and my mother and grandmother shared a Murphy bed in the alcove. I missed my father terribly. He . . . could fly down to see us just once a month. But I loved the freedom I had in Miami Beach."[12]

She started taking ballet lessons, played outside every night until dark, roller-skated to music at Flamingo Park, and went to the beach every weekend. "Even my anxious and overprotective mother seemed more relaxed in Florida."[13]

Her time in the Sunshine State would later be the inspiration for *Starring Sally J. Freedman As Herself,* about a ten year-old Jewish girl growing up in the late 1940s who finds the world a very scary, and exciting, place—just as Judy had. Even though only seven years old when the war ended, she says, "The war had so colored my early life it was hard to think of anything else."[14]

During World War II, Judy's dad had done his part for the war effort by volunteering as an air warden. It was his responsibility to take people to a safe place in the event of an air raid attack on Elizabeth by the Japanese or Germans. "As I listened to my parents whispering in the darkness, I couldn't help worrying that it could happen again," Judy says. "And this time the bombs could drop on our houses." Most frightening was the looming spectre of Hitler. "Never mind that Adolf Hitler was supposedly dead. I knew that he'd wanted to kill all the Jews in the world. And I was a Jew."[15]

> *How old are you?* the Head of Volunteers asks. I'm ten, Sally tells her, but I'm smart . . . and strong . . . and tough. Okay, I'm going to take a chance and send you . . . your ship leaves in an hour. Sally salutes, slings her duffle bag over her shoulder and boards the ship. . . . When they get home Sally is a hero. There is a big parade in her honor on Broad Street and everyone cheers. The people watching from the windows in the office buildings threw confetti, the way Sally did when Admiral Halsey came home at the end of the war.
>
> —*Starring Sally J. Freedman As Herself*

Like Sally, Judy's fantasy life offered an escape from her real-life fears. "My father was the youngest of seven siblings, all of whom died young," she says. "By the time I was ten I'd seen my father lose a sister, two brothers, and his mother. We were always sitting *shivah*. His two brothers died at 43, the age he was. I thought it was up to me to protect my father, and I invented fancy rituals to keep him safe. I grew up making all kinds of bargains with God. I never told anyone about this. It was a heavy burden for a child."[16]

And not one she felt free to talk about with her parents or brother. "We didn't talk about problems in our family. We kept our feelings to ourselves . . . like most children, I sometimes felt alone."[17]

Through her ten-year-old eyes, Judy saw, "A world of secrets kept from children, a world of questions without answers. Sally's family is based on my own. When I was nine and ten I was a lot like Sally—curious, imaginative, a worrier. In my stories I was brave and strong. I led a life of drama, adventure and fame. I think the character of Sally explains how and even why I became a writer."[18]

When Judy's family finally moved back to Elizabeth, she was in fourth grade and had almost magically overcome her shyness and became much more outgoing. "I can't explain the change," she admits, other than to observe she was "a late developer."[19]

Even though she still enjoyed making up her stories, friends became the center of Judy's world. "I still had the fantasies, the secrets, the imaginative life," Blume says, but it was increasingly important to be with her friends. She recalls eating dinner "as fast as you could get away with it and go back outside and play."[20]

Other escapes were going to the movies and reading. "I loved browsing at the public library. I was always reading something. Basically, I read whatever I could find. I not only liked the pictures and the stories, but also the feel and the smell of the books. . . . Books opened up a whole new world to me. Through them, I discovered new ideas, traveled to new places, and met new people. Books helped me learn to understand other people and they taught me a lot about myself."[21]

Her favorite books included the Betsy-Tacy series by Maud Hart Lovelace, which was about two best friends growing up in a small Minnesota town. Judy also enjoyed the Oz series, Nancy Drew mysteries and, especially, Madeline, which she loved so much that she hid the book so her mother couldn't return it to the library.

"Even after the overdue notices came, I didn't tell my mother where the book was," Blume recalled in a recent letter to the Ashland Public Library. "If only I had asked, I'm sure she would have bought me my own copy, but I didn't know that was a possibility then. I thought the copy I had hidden was the only copy in the whole world. I knew it was wrong to hide the book, but there was no way I was going to part with Madeline."[22]

Always hungry for new books to read, Judy saved her allowance so she could buy a book every week at Elizabeth's Ritz Bookstore. Although her parents were book lovers and had shelves of books in their living room, Judy says "It's funny, I don't think my parents read to me very often."[23]

Blume believes it very important for parents to read to, and with, their children. "I read to my children and now to my grandson," she says. "He loves being read to at bedtime, even though he's just learned to read. You should never stop reading aloud."[24]

A BURNING CURIOSITY

Are you there God? It's me, Margaret. I just told my mother I want a bra. Please help me grow God. You know where. I want to be like everyone else.

—Are You There God? It's Me, Margaret

Around sixth grade, when Judy was twelve, she noticed some girls in her class looked different . . . more mature. Those were the ones who had started their periods and, in Judy's mind, were on the road to becoming women. She wondered when it would happen to her and what the experience would be like.

"I had a lot of questions but I was afraid to ask them," she admits. "I was curious about sex but no one gave me any information. . . . I looked it up in the encyclopedia but all I found were pages and pages of plants and how they reproduce. . . . Even though I was envied for having a warm and loving father, one who claimed I could talk to him about anything, I never actually asked him the questions I had. I waited for him to tell me."[25]

And even when she was given information, she either didn't understand what he was saying or it seemed suspiciously incomplete. She remembers the time her father uncomfortably explained the nuts and bolts of where babies came from with "some sort of explanation about the seed and the egg and then something about intercourse."[26]

Judy later joked that all she took away from the conversation was that "whenever the moon was full, women all over the world were menstruating."[27]

In an online chat with gurl.com, Blume recalled, "My mother said nothing about anything, ever, which may have been not so terrible in the long run because while she didn't say anything positive, she didn't say anything negative either. She just didn't say anything. . . .

"When I had children, I vowed that they would never have to go elsewhere for information about sexuality. . . . One reason that parents have trouble talking with their kids about sex," she says, "is that they don't know the facts themselves."[28]

Unable to get answers from their parents, Judy and her friends turned to each other. They made a pact that whoever started menstruating first had to tell the others what it was like—in detail. They understood what happened physically from their science classes; what they craved to know was how it felt emotionally; and to be seen by others as a young woman instead of as a child. So they did exercises in hopes of getting their breasts to grow into their first training bras.

When that didn't work, Judy occasionally stuffed her bra with toilet paper to look more developed. It wasn't that she was in a hurry to be an adult; she just wanted to fit in. "I was small and thin when thin wasn't in," she recalls. "I was a late developer and was anxious to grow like my friends."[29] When twelve, she told all her friends she had started her period and even wore pads—although she wouldn't really begin menstruating until she was fourteen.

"You pretend like everybody else, I'm normal," Judy recalls. "But inside you know you're not and the harder you try to be. And you are afraid to be yourself because there is no yourself. You don't even know who yourself is."[30]

> I took off my dress and put on the bra. I fastened it first around my waist, then wiggled it up to where it belonged. I threw my shoulders back and stood sideways. I didn't look any different. I took out a pair of socks and stuffed one sock into each side of the bra, to see if it really grew with me. It was too tight that way, but I liked the way it looked.
>
> —*Are You There God? It's Me, Margaret*

Judy eventually caught up to her classmates and by high school was a typical teenager—which she says was not necessarily such a good thing. "I'm not that crazy about the teenager I was," Judy admits. "I much prefer the interesting person I was—to me, anyway—before I was a teen. As a teen, well, it was in the fifties, a very boring era. But as a ten year-old I had a depth and curiosity that still interests me. Maybe that happens to all of us. We're too into being like everyone else. Too concerned about how we look to our peers when we're teens."[31]

Judy attended Battin High School, the only all-girls public high school in New Jersey. "We complained a lot about being separated from the boys," she says, "but I'm not so sure it wasn't a good experience. We ran the school!"[32]

A good student whose favorite subjects were English and drama, Judy was outgoing and enjoyed participating in extracurricular activities. She sang with the chorus, danced in the modern dance troupe, auditioned for school plays, and "had great fun with my friends." Her only regret is that she didn't learn more. "Only one or two teachers encouraged us to think for ourselves, which I consider the most important part of any education. Only a few challenged us intellectually. Those are the teachers I remember best, the ones I respect most."[33]

Like many adolescents, Judy says her teen years were often filled with secret angst. "I was happy on the outside but I had a lot of anxiety on the inside."[34] The one person she was able to share her feelings with was her best friend Mary Weaver, nee Sullivan.

> Vix hung back, watching, as if she were in sixth grade again, studying Caitlin for the secret to success. . . . Caitlin was dazzling at seventeen. Her hair cascaded down her back, her skin

was moist and flawless, and the expression on her face dared anyone to mess with her. She'd reached her full height that year, leaving Vix three inches behind. . . . The boys drooled over her. Even the teachers found her irresistible.

—*Summer Sisters*

Judy met Mary in seventh grade homeroom and to this day considers Weaver her soul mate. "We became a team, best friends through junior high, high school and into college. Twins separated at birth—identical in size—one with a beautiful Irish face, the other a Jewish girl with a pony tail. Inseparable."[35]

They shared an interest in theater and both dreamed of being an actress. They were also co-feature editors of Battin's school newspaper. "Being together was so damn much fun," Judy says. "We felt so smug with our quick repartee and our private jokes."[36]

Esther Sussman approved her daughter's friendship with Weaver, in part because she deduced that Mary and Judy would not be competing for the same boyfriend. "My mother, who wanted me to be perfect, recognized Mary's beauty and winning personality but didn't feel threatened because Mary wasn't Jewish," Judy explains. "When I look back now and think of the times I lied to my mother to please her, to assure her that yes, indeed, I was the most popular, best all round girl, I cringe. I kept my anxieties to myself. Only my eczema gave me away."[37]

While Judy's parents might not have been communicative when it came to sex, they gave her plenty of freedom and privacy when it came to her social life. The Sussman house was a favorite hang-out spot with her friends because it had a piano, a jukebox, and a "make-out" room where in junior high she invited groups of boy and girls over for parties. They would turn out the lights and played kissing games. She also remembers playing basketball with guys in junior high who would occasionally tackle the girls in the group. Judy says it was "very exciting. And wonderful."[38]

When Judy was fifteen she started dating a college sophomore named Bernie. Although they dated for six years, she was not exclusive with Bernie and dated several other boys as well. She didn't have a strict curfew, although her parents insisted she come to their room and check in when she got home from a date. Judy says she was a typical 1950s Good Girl. The biggest risk she took was the night she and her date pulled off the road with the intention of making out.

"Just once, I wanted to know what it would feel like to make out in a car," and by that she means kissing, light petting, "whatever you want to call it."[39] But the car had barely come to a stop before a policeman appeared at the car window, shone his flashlight in and demanded to know how old Judy was.

"I thought, Oh, no—*good girl strays for half a second and is immediately caught*," Blume says, the irony being, "I wasn't doing anything! I mean, we had just pulled off the road!"[40] But to her great relief, the policeman didn't drag her home to her parents. He just warned the young couple not to park because it was dangerous.

Despite her curiosity about sex, Judy remained a virgin in high school. For one thing, she was scared of getting pregnant. For another, she wasn't ready. "Nobody ever pushed me. But that doesn't mean I wasn't sexual. I always enjoyed sexuality. But nobody was ever going to push me, and nobody ever tried to push me."[41]

It would be several more years before Judy lost her virginity. By then she was engaged to be married and looking forward to happily ever after. Except it didn't work out the way she planned.

NOTES

1. Nancy Shulins, "Despite Controversy, Judy Blume Gaining Fans," *AP Newsfeatures*, March 31, 1985, http://www.newspaperarchive.com/PdfViewer.aspx?img=26797522&firstvisit=true&src=search&currentResult=1&currentPage=0.

2. William Leith, "Teen Spirit," *The Independent (London)*, July 18, 1999, http://www.highbeam.com/doc/1P2–5001703.html.

3. Jennifer Frey, "Fiction Heroine," *Washington Post*, November 17, 2004, C1.

4. Tracy Chevalier, ed., *Twentieth Century Children Writers* (New York: St. James Press, 1989).

5. Judy Blume, "Judy Answers Your Favorite Questions About Personal Things," http://www.judyblume.com/ans-personal.html (accessed July 13, 2007).

6. Jennifer Frey, "Fiction Heroine," *Washington Post*, November 17, 2004, C1.

7. Scholastic.com. "Authors & Books." Judy Blume (location on the Web site). http://www2.scholastic.com/browse/collateral.jsp?id=10560&FullBreadCrumb=%3Ca+href%3D%22%2Fbrowse%2Fsearch.jsp%3Fquery%3Djudy+blume%26c1%3DCONTENT30%26c17%3D0%26c2%3Dfalse%22%3EAll+Results+%3C%2Fa%3E (accessed July 13, 2007).

8. KidsRead.com. Judy Blume http://www.kidsreads.com/authors/au-blume-judy.asp (accessed July 13, 2007).

9. Press material from Random House http://www.randomhouse.com/features/blume/scrapbook.html.

10. Ibid.

11. Connie G. Rockman, ed., *Eighth Book of Junior Authors and Illustrators* (New York: H. W. Wilson, 2000.

12. Ibid.

13. Ibid.

14. Judy Blume, *Starring Sally J Freedman as Herself*, http://www.judyblume. com/sally.html (accessed July 13, 2007).

15. Ibid.

16. Judy Freeman, "Talking with Judy Blume," *Instructor*, May 1, 2005, http:// www.highbeam.com/doc/1G1–132531055.html.

17. Agnes Garrett and Helga P. McCue, *Authors and Artists for Young Adults*, vol. 3 (Farmington Hills, Mich.: Thomson Gale), pp. 25–36.

18. Judy Blume, *Starring Sally J Freedman as Herself*, http://www.judyblume. com/sally.html (accessed July 13, 2007).

19. Press material from Random House http://www.randomhouse.com/features/ blume/scrapbook.html.

20. Jennifer Frey, "Fiction Heroine," *Washington Post*, November 17, 2004, C1.

21. Betsy Lee, *Judy Blume's Story* (Minneapolis: Dillon Press, 1977).

22. Matt McDonald, "Library Cherishes Far-Flung Pen Pals," *Globe West*, May 4, 2003, p. 14.

23. Scholastic.com, "Authors & Books," Judy Blume (location on the Web site), http://www2.scholastic.com/browse/collateral.jsp?id=10560&FullBreadCr umb=%3Ca+href%3D%22%2Fbrowse%2Fsearch.jsp%3Fquery%3Djudy+blume %26c1%3DCONTENT30%26c17%3D0%26c2%3Dfalse%22%3EAll+Results+ %3C%2Fa%3E (accessed July 13, 2007).

24. Ibid.

25. MSNBC.com., "Literary Lightning Rod," *Newsweek*, http://www.msnbc. msn.com/id/18725395/site/newsweek (accessed July 13, 2007).

26. William Leith, "Teen Spirit," *The Independent (London,)* July 18, 1999, http://www.highbeam.com/doc/1P2–5001703.html.

27. Peter Gorner, "The Giddy/Sad, Flighty/Solid Life Of Judy Blume," *Chicago Tribune*, March 15, 1985, p. 1.

28. William Leith, "Teen Spirit," *The Independent (London)*, July 18, 1999, http://www.highbeam.com/doc/1P2–5001703.html.

29. Scholastic.com, "Authors & Books," Judy Blume (location on the Web site), http://www2.scholastic.com/browse/collateral.jsp?id=10560&FullBreadCr umb=%3Ca+href%3D%22%2Fbrowse%2Fsearch.jsp%3Fquery%3Djudy+blume %26c1%3DCONTENT30%26c17%3D0%26c2%3Dfalse%22%3EAll+Results+ %3C%2Fa%3E (accessed July 13, 2007).

30. Cee Telford, *Judy Blume* (New York: Rosen Publishing. 2004), pg. 8.

31. Scholastic.com, "Authors & Books," Judy Blume (location on Web site), http://www2.scholastic.com/browse/collateral.jsp?id=10560&FullBreadCr umb=%3Ca+href%3D%22%2Fbrowse%2Fsearch.jsp%3Fquery%3Djudy+blume %26c1%3DCONTENT30%26c17%3D0%26c2%3Dfalse%22%3EAll+Results+ %3C%2Fa%3E (accessed July 13, 2007).

32. Connie G. Rockman, ed., *Eighth Book of Junior Authors and Illustrators* (New York: H. W. Wilson, 2000).

33. Ibid.

34. "Author Profile: Judy Blume," Teenreads.com, http://www.teenreads.com/authors/au-blume-judy.asp (accessed July 13, 2007).

35. Judy Blume, "Best Friends," *She Still Knows You Best: Judy Blume Scrapbook,* http://www.randomhouse.com/features/blume/scrapbook.html (accessed July 13, 2007).

36. Ibid.

37. Ibid.

38. William Leith, "Teen Spirit," *The Independent (London)*, July 18, 1999, http://www.highbeam.com/doc/1P2–5001703.htm.

39. Ibid.

40. Ibid.

41. Ibid.

Chapter 2

A TRADITIONAL WIFEY

Judy graduated from Battin High School with honors at the top of her class and enrolled at Boston University. But just two weeks after the semester started, Judy contracted mononucleosis, a viral infection that causes intense fatigue. Unable to attend class, Judy had to withdraw. When she was finally ready to go back, she decided against returning to Boston and enrolled at New York University instead. "I wanted to become an elementary school teacher and to find a husband," she says. "That's what was expected of most young women back then."[1]

During her sophomore year, Judy met a law student named John Blume. After dating for ten months, John proposed. But just weeks before her wedding, Judy's dad died unexpectedly. Her lifelong fear that he would die young came heartbreakingly true. In part, Judy blames Rudolph's lifelong addiction to nicotine and never misses an opportunity to discourage young people from picking up the habit. "Let me tell you, it is not cool to smoke. It's disgusting. My father died when I was 21. He was a very heavy smoker, so I urge you not to smoke."[2]

Judy and John were married on August 15, 1959. It should have been one of the happiest days of her life; instead, Judy's heart was heavy with sorrow because her father wasn't there to walk her down the aisle and give her away. Years later she would say it had taught her that life makes you pay to be happy.

Judy earned a degree in education but never worked as a teacher because by the time she graduated, she was already pregnant with her first child. Their daughter, Randy Lee, was born in 1961 and their second child, Lawrence Andrew, was born two years later. John seemed content with their life. "He had married this little girl, and he was happy that way,"[3] Judy observes, while she was plagued by a growing restlessness. It occurred to Judy that of all the things she had fantasized about becoming back when she was ten, being a stay-at-home mom had not been one of them. "Somewhere along the way, my mother's wishes for me—a good husband and a good provider—became my way of life. I didn't resent it; I only had second thoughts about it later."[4]

As a freshman in college, Judy and her roommate had bought a copy of *Love Without Fear: How to Achieve Sex Happiness in Marriage*. But finding intimacy and sexual fulfillment in real life was proving more difficult than simply reading a book. "By the time I was twenty-five I had two small children. I had a degree in education, but I never taught. I lived in a house in suburban New Jersey in a neighborhood not that different from the one in which I grew up. I loved my little children, but I wasn't really happy."[5] Her anxiety expressed itself in rashes and allergies.

To others it appeared that Judy had a happy life. She had a successful husband, two healthy kids, and a comfortable home. But inside, Judy felt as if she were withering away. "It was a nice marriage," she says, "but I was dying."[6]

> "Oh, San, for God's sake." He tried to put his arms around her but she brushed him away. "You're so damned *touchy* these days," he said, "I can't even talk to you anymore."
>
> *Anymore?* Sandy thought. But she didn't say it.
>
> As soon as she heard the back door close she picked up a plate and flung it across the kitchen. It smashed into tiny pieces. She felt better.
>
> —*Wifey*

Judy's emotional malaise was exacerbated by not having Mary in her life as much. She was lonely in her marriage and missed the closeness of her best friend. "I was constantly hoping to find someone with whom I could connect. Each time a moving van brought a new family to our cul-de-sac, I'd be out there, a welcome committee of one, hoping this would be it. It never was."[7]

Judy and Mary had slowly drifted apart after their respective marriages. Even though they had daughters born only two months apart, Blume says their lives had become very different. Mary lived in New York and Judy in suburban New Jersey. "Her husband, a Wasp who came from old money, was an academic; mine was a hustling young lawyer," Blume says. "The men had nothing in common."[8]

Although she and Mary stayed in touch and never stopped being friends, "We just didn't get to spend much time together and when we tried it as a foursome it never really worked. I felt the loss of that friendship."[9]

She also felt trapped and sensed the world was passing her by. She had gotten married at 21 in the conservative 1950s, when men were considered the sole breadwinners and women were expected to defer to their husbands. By the time she was 25, Blume was a homemaker, mother of two. At first, she just accepted her life because "in those days, we all did that." But then everything changed. The 1960s Cultural Revolution happened: there were anti-Vietnam war demonstrations, demands for civil rights, a push for female equality and a call for more openness when it came to our bodies and our sexuality. Judy desperately wanted to be a part of it. "I wanted to go to Woodstock. I wanted to be active in the women's movement and the sexual revolution."[10]

Instead, she was a housewife in Scotch Plains, New Jersey, who played tennis and kept a clean house. Just as she had as a child, Judy kept her problems to herself, unable to talk about them with anyone, especially her mother. "My mother is still tuned into *Are you happy?* That's always the first question," and Judy says she tried desperately to keep up the pretense that everything was going well in her life and marriage. She could never admit "to the pain or disappointment I might have been feeling."[11]

> Is this what my life is all about? Driving the kids to and from school and decorating our final house? Oh Mother, dammit! Why did you bring me up to think this was what I wanted?
>
> —*Wifey*

It was clear something vital was missing from Judy's life: "an outlet for my creative energy."[12] To fill the void, she began considering career options. To her credit, Judy never considered failure. She credits her time at Battin High School. "There was nothing we felt we couldn't do as girls."[13]

For a while she tried songwriting. Then she created decorative felt picture banners for children's rooms in her basement. "Being naive, I put them in a suitcase and went to Bloomingdale's," she recalls. "They paid me $9 each, and then I sat in my basement and waited for special orders. I finally had to give it up because I was allergic to the glue."[14]

The banners had been a diversion but hadn't fulfilled Judy the way she craved. She tried to remember what had appealed to her growing up and the more she thought, the more she realized the one thing she loved to do more than almost anything was to make up stories inside her head.

Even as a married mom of two toddlers, Judy would make up rhyming stories while washing dishes, sometimes daydreaming about being the next Dr. Seuss.

As a kid it had never occurred to Judy that she could grow up to be a writer. "That's because no one ever told me there was such a thing," she says. "When I was growing up, you could be a nurse or a teacher. I used to dream of being a movie star, but that's because I knew they existed."[15]

As an adult, though, one thing was very clear. "When I grew up, my need for story telling didn't go away. So when my own two children started pre-school I began to write. . . .[16] I started to write, out of loneliness, maybe even desperation." Growing up, Judy had always thought it would be Mary who would have the interesting career, but she says, "I was the ambitious one, driven and determined, though I didn't know it at the time."[17]

THE WRITER EMERGES

From the outset, Judy wrote stories for children, mostly because it never occurred to her to write anything else. Plus, she says when she looks back at her youth, "[T]hose are the years that are the most real and full of emotion." By contrast, Blume's not fond of who she was as a teen. She considers that person "boring. . . . She's beginning to get to be like everyone else. . . . What happened to that other kid, the one who was really excited about life?"[18] Judy muses that even though she was a twenty-eight year-old woman when she began writing, she continued to see the world through the eyes of a twelve-year-old because emotionally, she was still a child. "I didn't know anything about being a grown-up, even though I was married and had two babies. . . .[19] I wrote children's books because I was a child; a baby. I didn't really connect to that other world—I had no experience as an adult . . .[20]

"So I wrote what I knew. And what I really knew about was being a kid. It never occurred to me to write anything but children's books; I had this deep need."[21]

Another thing that appealed to her about adolescence was it was a time of endless possibility. "When you're 12, you're on the brink of adulthood but everything is still in front of you, and you still have the chance to be almost anyone you want. That seemed so appealing to me. I wasn't even 30 when I started writing, but already I didn't feel I had much chance myself."[22]

For the next two years, Judy wrote several stories on her old college typewriter and tried unsuccessfully to have them published. She did not find much support at home. John didn't take her attempt to be a writer seriously; he saw it as just the hobby of a housewife to pass the time.

"When I started to write, my husband thought it was very cute," Blume says. "He thought all he had to do was buy me paper and pencils, like a new box of Crayolas, and I'd be happy. I kept it inside, but what I was doing was not a joke. It was very important to me."[23] Judy also reveals that for much of her child-rearing years she was frequently physically ill and believes without that outlet she would have literally fallen emotionally apart.

Others tried to actively discourage her. "My then-husband had a best friend who was an English major at college," Judy recalls. "He said, *You're a nice girl, Judy, but you can't write*. Also, I sent an early manuscript to someone who wrote picture books and he said, *Give it up. You have no talent*."[24]

The lack of support and encouragement filled Judy with self-doubt. "At night I would think, *I'll never get anything published*. But in the morning I'd wake up and say, *I can do this*. It's hard to deal with rejection, but if you write it's a fact of life."[25]

Finally, Judy felt she needed some instruction to hone her abilities. As fate would have it, she received a brochure in the mail from NYU and saw a class being offered called "Writing for Children and Teenagers." The instructor was Jane Andrews Lee Hyndman—better known by her pseudonym Lee Wyndham, a children's author popular in the 1940s and 1950s. Blume enrolled and knew she was right where she needed to be. Wyndham became the first person who ever actively encouraged her to write.

"While I believe that no one can teach you how to write," Judy says, "I needed professional encouragement (especially after two years of rejection letters) and found it in that class. When the semester ended, I signed up and took the course again."[26]

The classes had become a focal point of her week. She would take a commuter train to Manhattan, then have dinner by herself in the city before going to class. For the first time in her adult life, she felt truly independent. But perhaps the most important thing Judy learned in the writing class was to stay true to her own writing voice. Wyndham's instruction included very strictly defined rules on how children's stories should be written, but Blume admits thinking, "Never mind these rules. This isn't what it's really like."[27] It wasn't that she was out to redefine children's stories; she was simply driven to write honestly about feelings and situations she had personally experienced and knew to be true.

In 1966, Judy sold her first stories—*The Flying Munchkins* and *The Ooh-ooh-aah Bird*. The first book she finished, which was aimed at younger children, was *You, Mom, You?* That went unpublished. In retrospect, Blume admits those early efforts make her cringe when she thinks about them now. "I sent out such junk. I put picture books together with brass fasteners and sent them off to publishers. Then I sat around having all these wonderful fantasies."[28]

But she kept writing and finally an illustrated children's book called *The One in the Middle Is the Green Kangaroo* was published by Reilly and Lee in 1969. "There's never been a day to equal that one,"[29] she says, remembering the day she found out the book had sold. In the thirty-three-page story, second grader Freddy Dissel is the middle of three kids in his family and feels invisible. His older brother and baby sister seem to get all the attention, leaving him to be the forgotten "peanut butter between two pieces of bread," as Peter says. When Freddy is given the role of a green kangaroo in a school play, he finally gets the chance to show how special he is.

Although she provided drawings for the *Green Kangaroo* manuscript, Judy quickly realized she should stick with writing. "I tried to illustrate my first efforts but I'm totally not an illustrator so it was sort of a joke."[30] Amy Aitkin was eventually hired to provide the illustrations. After *Green Kangaroo*'s release, a local paper ran an article about Judy with the head-line: "Mom Keeps Busy Writing Books for Little Children," making it sounds as if writing was still just a pastime and not a passion.

That same year, she finished her first full-length work, *Iggie's House*. The book examined racial prejudice through the story of a black family moving into an all-white neighborhood, a topic that was very much in the forefront of social issues in the late 1960s and early 1970s. Blume says she got the idea by simply looking down her own Scotch Plains street.

> I lived in a neighborhood in suburban New Jersey that was all white, and I liked to think about how the neighbors would handle a racially mixed neighborhood. It was the very begin-ning of the seventies and I wanted my kids to know kids of all backgrounds.[31]

Before she finished *Iggie's*, Judy had read in a magazine about a new publishing company called Bradbury Press that was seeking realistic books about childhood and adolescence. She called the number in the ad and arranged a meeting with Dick Jackson. He eventually offered her a deal to publish *Iggie's House* and Bradbury would later reissue *Green Kangaroo*.

Writing gave Judy a fulfillment that had been missing in her life. "A creative child grows up, and then what? If you come of age at a time when you're not supposed to do anything but be a good wifey, what are you sup-posed to do with it?" For many years she tried to live up to those expecta-tions. "I tried to fit in." But she never did.[32]

But writing gave her a place to belong. Having *Green Kangaroo* and *Iggie's House* published gave Judy the confidence she needed to take her writing to a deeper level. She remembers telling herself, "Now that I've figured out how to write books I'm going to write what I know to be true."[33]

Judy used the money from her first sale to buy an electric typewriter and set out to write her next book. Over the next five years, her commitment to honesty would bring Judy success and fame as a writer. But as her professional life flourished, her personal life with her husband would become irrevocably broken.

NOTES

1. Connie G. Rockman, ed., *Eighth Book of Junior Authors and Illustrators* (New York: H. W. Wilson, 2000).

2. William Leith, "Interview: Teen Spirit," *The Independent (London)*, July 18, 1999, http://findarticles.com/p/articles/mi_qn4158/is_19990718/ai_n14242010.

3. Peter Gorner, "The Giddy/Sad, Flighty/Solid Life Of Judy Blume," *Chicago Tribune*, March 15, 1985, p. 1.

4. Enid Nemy, "It's Judy Blume, New Yorker," *New York Times*, October 3, 1982, http://select.nytimes.com/search/restricted/article?res=F30711FB345C0C708CDDA90994DA484D81

5. Connie G. Rockman, ed., *Eighth Book of Junior Authors and Illustrators* (New York: H.W. Wilson, 2000).

6. Richard Flaste, "Viewing Childhood as It Is," *New York Times*, September 29, 1976, http://select.nytimes.com/mem/archive/pdf?res=F40F1EFE3B58167493CBAB1782D85F428785F9.

7. Judy Blume, "Best Friends," *She Still Knows You Best: Judy Blume Scrapbook*, http://www.randomhouse.com/features/blume/scrapbook.html (accessed July 13, 2007).

8. Ibid.

9. Ibid.

10. Jennifer Frey, "Fiction Heroine," *Washington Post*, November 17, 2004, C1.

11. Sandy Rovner, "Judy Blume: Talking It Out," *Washington Post*, November 3, 1981, B1.

12. Connie G. Rockman, ed., *Eighth Book of Junior Authors and Illustrators* (New York: H. W. Wilson, 2000).

13. Enid Nemy, "It's Judy Blume, New Yorker," *New York Times*, October 3, 1982, http://select.nytimes.com/search/restricted/article?res=F30711FB345C0C708CDDA90994DA484D81.

14. Ibid.

15. Brooks Whitney, "Judy Blume Gets Real. She Wrote the Book on Growing Pains," *Chicago Tribune*, November 23, 1993.

16. Press material from Random House.

17. Judy Blume, "Best Friends," *She Still Knows You Best: Judy Blume Scrapbook*, http://www.randomhouse.com/features/blume/scrapbook.html (accessed July 13, 2007).

18. Randy Sue Coburn, "A Best-Selling But Much-Censored Author," *San Francisco Chronicle*, August 12, 1985, p. 15.

19. Peter Gorner, "The Giddy/Sad, Flighty/Solid Life Of Judy Blume," *Chicago Tribune*, March 15, 1985, p. 1.

20. Nancy Shulins, "Despite controversy, Judy Blume Gaining Fans," *AP Newsfeatures*, March 31, 1985, http://www.newspaperarchive.com/PdfViewer.aspx?img=26797522&firstvisit=true&src=search&currentResult=1&currentPage=0.

21. Peter Gorner, "The Giddy/Sad, Flighty/Solid Life Of Judy Blume," *Chicago Tribune*, March 15, 1985, p. 1.

22. Judy (Sussman) Blume, *Major Authors and Illustrators for Children and Young Adults*, 2nd ed., 8 vols. (Farmington Hills, Mich.:Thomson Gale, 2002).

23. Cynthia Roberts, "Judy Blume: No More Kids' Stuff," *Chronicle-Telegram*, October 20, 1978, http://www.newspaperarchive.com/PdfViewer.aspx?img=29965503&firstvisit=true&src=search&currentResult=2&currentPage=0.

24. Scholastic.com. "Authors & Books." Judy Blume (location on the Web site). http://www2.scholastic.com/browse/collateral.jsp?id=105b0_type=contributor_typeId=1310 (accessed September 3, 2007)..

25. Ibid.

26. Connie G. Rockman, ed., *Eighth Book of Junior Authors and Illustrators* (New York: H. W. Wilson, 2000).

27. Herbert N. Foerstel, *Banned in the U.S.A.: A Reference Guide to Book Censorship in Schools and Public Libraries* (Westport: Greenwood Press, 2002), p. 134.

28. Nancy Shulins, "Despite Controversy, Judy Blume Gaining Fans," *AP Newsfeatures*, March 31, 1985.

29. Ibid.

30. Linda Richards, "Judy Blume: On Censorship, Enjoying Life, and Staying in the Spotlight for 25 years," *January Magazine*,1998 http://januarymagazine.com/profiles/blume.html.

31. Scholastic.com. "Authors & Books." Judy Blume (location on the Web site). http://www2.scholastic.com/teachers/authorsandbooks/authorstudies/authorhome.jhtml (accessed September 3, 2007) .

32. Jennifer Frey, "Fiction Heroine," *Washington Post*, November 17, 2004, C1.

33. Herbert N. Foerstel, *Banned in the U.S.A.: A Reference Guide to Book Censorship in Schools and Public Libraries* (Westport: Greenwood Press, 2002), p. 134.

Chapter 3

THE VOICE OF YOUTH

Judy Blume's third book, *Are You There God? It's Me, Margaret,* took readers inside the world of Margaret Simon, an eleven soon-to-be twelve-year-old at a crossroads in her life. First, her family has just moved from the city into the suburbs, so Margaret is trying to fit in at her new school and make new friends while adjusting to suburbia. Then there's the matter of religion—she doesn't have one. At least, not officially. Margaret's parents—a Christian mother and Jewish father—decided to let her choose which religion to follow and Margaret is still undecided. Not having a religion makes her feel even more an outcast. The issue is also causing problems with her maternal grandparents, who make it clear they want Margaret to be Christian. Margaret's paternal grandmother is more accepting of her son's interfaith marriage and through visits to the synagogue shows Margaret about Judaism.

Rounding off Margaret's problems is her preoccupation with her body, worrying about when she'll ever finally start her period and wondering what her body will look like as she grows older. Through it all, Margaret maintains a running dialogue with God, the only time she can comfortably voice all her anxieties and fears. "Margaret's relationship to God is based on mine at her age," Blume reveals, "God as friend, God as confidante."[1]

> Are you there God? It's me, Margaret. Gretchen, my friend, got her period. I'm so jealous, God. I hate myself for being so jealous, but I am. I wish you'd help me just a little. Nancy's sure

she's going to get it soon, too. And if I'm the last I don't know what I'll do. Oh please God, I just want to be normal.

—*Are You There God? It's Me, Margaret.*

Judy had no idea she was writing anything revolutionary; she was simply writing a story that included her own experiences in sixth grade. "I didn't know anything," Blume stresses. "I was really young and naive and inexperienced. I would write what I knew to be true from my own experience growing up.[2] For the first time since I'd started writing, I let go and this story came pouring out."[3]

The story also caused a shock wave. Before *Margaret*, talking about menstruation in a mainstream, fiction book was considered practically taboo. Kathleen O'Grady, a feminist historian who wrote the book *Sweet Secrets: Stories of Menstruation* in 1997, says, "In the generation before Judy Blume, a huge number of women thought when they had their first menstruation that they were dying. They had very little information. Prior to widespread TV advertisements about sanitary protection, there weren't a huge number of sources. Judy Blume, I think, really opened up discussion in that area."[4]

In *The Body Project: An Intimate History of American Girls*, by Joan Jacobs Brumberg, there were many in the medical community during the late nineteenth century that asserted menstruation was a new phenomenon. An 1895 study revealed that 60 percent of high school girls in Boston did not know what a period was so that when it began, they were terrified because they did not know what was happening to them.

O'Grady unearthed one of the more fascinating cases that highlights just how unmentionable the subject was by while researching her book. In the 1990s, a new edition of *The Diary of Anne Frank* was released, boasting never before included entries that Anne's father, Otto, had insisted be censored.

"I thought it would have to be something horrific, something to do with the Holocaust, but it turned out what had been censored out were passages about menstruation," O'Grady says, incredulous. "We can give young kids books in school about the Holocaust, but we can't let them know about menstruation."[5]

UNEXPECTED CONTROVERSY

Judy was more than a little surprised when *Margaret* was singled out for its ground-breaking content. "It was not courage. It was naiveté," she says. "I had absolutely no idea I was writing a controversial book. There was nothing in it that wasn't a part of my sixth grade experience."[6]

While Blume's intention was not to write brave books, she does stress she intended to write honest ones. Growing up, Judy longed to find characters in books she could identify with, so when she began to write, "I wanted to write the kinds of books that weren't there for me."[7]

Judy recalls the day her publisher called and read *Margaret's* glowing review in the *New York Times* over the phone. "I had a tennis racket in my hand—I was still being the dutiful suburban wife. I put that tennis racket down and sank to my knees."[8]

Looking back, Blume says, "That book brought me my first readers who went on to become some of my most loyal readers. And they've followed me through everything that I've written since. So that book was the first book that I wrote from deep inside. I published two books before it, but with *Margaret* I really let go." It was also the book "that made me feel I might actually become a writer."[9]

Margaret's success prompted Blume to finally hire an agent and brought her first fan letters. "In 1971 I received my first letter from a young reader. She was 13 and she wrote to tell me that she was exactly like the character of Margaret. I was surprised and thrilled, and I wrote back to her the same day." But the letters brought the sobering realization that she had become a role model for young girls. "Kids like to know that a parent—an adult—can remember," she says. "The trust is what gets me. The responsibility. It never occurred to me there'd be feedback."[10]

Margaret became so beloved that when Blume updated the book over twenty years later, some of her fans were stung. Judy is amazed at how upset people got over her decision to give Margaret modern day feminine hygiene products. "Some people said, *Oh, no, it's a classic. You can't mess around with a classic.* And I said, *Look, we're not messing around with the character or anything else.* It has nothing to do with the story—I have updated the equipment that Margaret uses," she says. Her intent was to simply make the book more factual and informative for current times. "No one uses belts any more. Half the mothers haven't used them," Blume notes, saying that current young readers "have to go to their grandmothers."[11]

Then, and now, despite how much young girls loved the book, some parents were furious. Regardless of whether Judy intended the book to be controversial or not, *Margaret* came under a withering attack from conservative social and religious groups. One went so far as to publish a brochure titled, "How to Rid Your Schools and Libraries of Judy Blume Books."[12] But initially, Judy was unaware of the backlash because her publishers shielded her from the negative letters and phone calls. Blume says her first clue that she had upset anyone was when "the principal of my children's school wouldn't put *Margaret* on the shelves . . . because she gets her period. Like, kids in elementary school don't get their periods. It's ludicrous. Even my friends way back then had their periods in sixth grade."[13]

Judy shrugged it off, thinking it was just an odd, isolated case. But it wasn't. She remembers the time "a woman called me on the phone and asked me if I had written *Are You There God? It's Me, Margaret.* When I said yes, she called me a communist and hung up." Blume jokes she never did figure out if the woman equated communism with menstruation or religion. But seriously, Judy said "I was bewildered and perplexed in the beginning, and I was personally hurt. Now I understand that this is something much bigger than any kind of personal attack on any one of us."[14]

It was the first time she fully understood the lengths some people would go to censor information, acting out of their own ignorance and fears. Such thinking was completely out of Judy's frame of reference because when she was growing up her father had an extensive library and her parents never told her what she could or couldn't read. "Not that my mother discussed the subjects in those books, but I never felt that I couldn't read them. My mother was very shy, but she was a reader, and reading was always considered a good thing in my house."[15]

Blume says she was also lucky that despite the backlash against *Margaret*, nobody suggested she change the way she wrote, partly because, she believes, the 1970s "were a much more open time. A time when people weren't afraid of taking chances: and I'm talking about the publishers and the editors. I had this wonderful young editor and publisher who never made me feel I was doing anything the least bit controversial. Because I didn't feel I was. And we were just lucky to all come together then."[16]

But even when the attacks against her books increased, Judy refused to back down. "*Margaret's* popularity over the years has proved to me that while the way we live may have changed, what's deep inside us hasn't."[17] And she was determined to continue writing about those universal emotions and experiences no matter how much criticism she received. Over the next four years, Judy wrote seven more books that touched on everything from bullying to freckles and, in *Then Again, Maybe I Won't*, wet dreams.

> When I read from Joel's paperbacks I can feel myself get hard. But other times when I'm not even thinking about anything it goes up too. I don't know what to do about that. I mean, if my brain is working right it's supposed to control my whole body. But if I don't have any control over that part of me what good is my brain? It's getting so I don't have anything to say about what goes on. I think that part of me has a mind of its own.
>
> —*Then Again, Maybe I Won't*

After she finished *Margaret*, Judy thought it would be interesting to write a book from a twelve-year-old boy's point of view. "I think it's great for boys to read about girls, and girls to read about boys," she says. "It's a great way to find out that you're not all that different, and the differences that you perceive, you know, hey, they're good ones."[18]

She gave the character, Tony Miglione, an unusual problem: his middle-class, Italian-American family is suddenly rich from an invention his father created. They move from their modest home in blue-collar Jersey City to a big house in a wealthy, upper-class suburban neighborhood. Tony's new friend, Joel, is a shoplifter. Joel's sixteen-year-old sister never bothers to draw the blinds when she takes her clothes off at night, giving Tony a clear view of her well-developed body.

But even though Tony is a little preoccupied with sex, he's more concerned with the changes he sees happening to his family. His grandmother has locked herself away in her room and his mother is so desperate to fit in with her rich neighbors that she downplays their Italian-American background. While the book is often remembered for letting readers know that wet dreams are a normal part of growing up for adolescent boys, the main underlying message of the book is the importance of staying true to yourself and your beliefs regardless of your surroundings.

Sometimes the real-life situations Judy wrote about were more silly than serious. In *Freckle Juice*, another illustrated book for younger children, Andrew sits behind a boy named Nicky in school. Nicky's face and neck are covered with freckles. It occurs to Andrew that if he had freckles, his mother wouldn't be able to tell whether or not his neck was dirty. And if she couldn't tell if his neck was dirty, he wouldn't have to wash it all the time. So when his classmate Sharon offers to sell him a secret recipe for freckles, Andrew accepts. . .

Blume says she got the idea for the book from her daughter Randy. "When she was small, she'd get into the bathtub at night and make a mess. She called this concoction Freckle Juice. It consisted of baby powder, shampoo, and anything else she could mix together. So I had to write a book with that title."[19]

It was one of the few times she started writing a book with the title already in mind. "Most of the time the title comes at the end," she says. "I always have trouble with titles for my books. I usually have no title until the editor has to present the book and calls me frantically. With *Are You There God? It's Me, Margaret*, I just took the first line. With *Then Again, Maybe I Won't*, I took the last." But unlike titles, "Character names pop into my head. I've no idea where they come from. But since I've written so many books, I sometimes use the phone book for names, too."[20]

Blume says she almost always comes up with the characters before she thinks of a story to go with them. "A good writer is always a people watcher. Observe. Make notes. Listen carefully. Listen to how people talk to one another. I'm really quite bad at coming up with plot ideas. I like to create characters and just see what will happen to them when I let them loose!"[21]

The characters live inside Judy's head for a long time before she actually starts a book about them. "Then, they become so real to me I talk about them at the dinner table as if they are real. Some people consider this weird," Blume admits. "But my family understands."[22]

Before she starts writing, Judy keeps a notebook about the characters, possible scenes, snippets of potential dialogue, background information on the character and their family—anything that helps being the book to life. "But even with my notebook," she says, "I still don't know everything. For me, finding out is the best part of writing."[23]

Judy admits that when she's writing a book, she creatively becomes that person; seeing the world through their eyes whether it's a boy or girl, young person or old. "Except I don't know sometimes what my characters will do until they do it. They surprise me. I think, *My God! I had no idea she'd do that!* After writing so many books now, I just tell myself to relax and let it come."[24]

She got the idea for her characters in *It's Not the End of the World* by seeing how many families in her suburban New Jersey neighborhood were being fractured by divorce. The central character in the book is twelve-year-old Karen Newman, whose family is slowly imploding. The only time her parents communicate is when they are arguing with each other. They no longer sleep in the same bed or have dinner together. When her father finally moves out, her mother expresses gleeful relief. Watching the two people she loves the most destroy each other convinces Karen that marriage only causes heartbreak and vows to remain single when she grows up. Even so, Karen does everything in her power to get her parents back together. But she ultimately has to grapple with the reality that sometimes two people, even if they love each other, can't live together anymore. . .

"As family after family split up, my kids became fearful that this could happen to us, too," Judy recalls. "I tried to reassure them, but I wasn't really sure myself."[25]

Blume wrote *End of the World* partly to address the concerns her children—and many other children—had about divorce, partly to let kids know they were not alone in their fears and because Judy was unhappy with her own marriage. "I kept those feelings deep inside. For years I would not, could not, admit that we had any problems. The perfect daughter had become the perfect wife and mother." Rather than confront John about her unhappiness, Judy kept silent. "In the hope that it would get better I dedicated this book to my husband."[26]

> I want my life back! Before it's too late. Or is it already too late? Is this it, then? Is this what my life is all about? Driving the kids to and from school and decorating our final house? Oh, Mother, dammit! Why did you bring me up to think *this* was what I wanted? And now that I know it's not, what am I supposed to do about it?
>
> —*Wifey*

Blume admits that while *End of the World* may have helped many children better cope with their parents' divorce, "It didn't help our family. Intellectually, you can understand what's happening, but emotionally, you get so involved in a situation that, while you know what you'd advise others, you can't do it yourself."[27]

Ironically, Judy believes her ability to vividly recreate adolescent experiences hindered her effectiveness as a parent. At the same time, she now thinks she was too hard on herself as a parent. "It's hard to be so aware of what your kids are thinking and feeling," she says. "I empathized too much."[28]

While Judy says she now has a close relationship with her son Larry and her daughter Randy, she says they can be very critical at times. "Sometimes they still treat me like a dunce, urging me to get in the shorter line at the bank, asking if I have my car keys . . ." Blume once asked how they thought she was incapable of finding her way to the doctor but managed to be competent enough to write books. "Randy thought about it a minute and finally shook her head and answered: *I don't know*."[29]

The truth was, Judy needed to write and over the next two years she would churn out four more best-sellers. "I've always been able to write, even when everything else was falling apart." And as her relationship with John grew ever more distant, Blume says bluntly, "Work really saved me."[30]

NOTES

1. "Judy Blume Looks Back," *People*, November 29, 2004, p. 59.

2. Ellen Barry, "Judy Blume for President," *The Boston Phoenix*, May 26, 1998, http://weeklywire.com/ww/05–26–98/boston_feature_1.html.

3. Ingram Library Services, *Ingram Explores: Summer Reading*, http://www.ingramlibrary.com/MRKNG/Explores/0307/explore.html.

4. Kathleen O'Grady and Paula Wansbrough, *Sweet Secrets: Stories of Menstruation* (Toronto: Second Story Press, 1997).

5. Ellen Barry, "Judy Blume for President," *The Boston Phoenix,* May 26, 1998, http://weeklywire.com/ww/05–26–98/boston_feature_1.html.

6. Herbert N. Foerstel, *Banned in the U.S.A.: A Reference Guide to Book Censorship in Schools and Public Libraries* (Westport: Greenwood Press, 2002), p. 134.

7. Amy Bryant, "Teenwire.com Talks with Judy Blume," May 22, 2007, http://www.teenwire.com/infocus/2007/if-20070522p487-blume.php. Used with Permission from Planned Parenthood Federation of America, Inc.

8. Nancy Shulins, "Despite Controversy, Judy Blume Gaining Fans," *AP Newsfeatures,* March 31, 1985.

9. Michelle Norris, "Judy Blume Discusses Her Career as a Successful and Controversial Author of Books for Young Readers," interview for National Public Radio, *All Things Considered,* September 15, 2004, http://www.highbeam.com/doc/1P1–107433907.html (accessed July 13, 2007).

10. Judy Blume, "Dear Judy, Letters Address Children's Secret Feelings," *Chicago Tribune,* May 4, 1986, Tempo Section, p. 1.

11. Rebecca Traister, "Modernizing Margaret," *Chicago Sun-Times,* March 8, 2006, http://www.highbeam.com/doc/1P2–1608650.html.

12. Herbert N. Foerstel, *Banned in the U.S.A.: A Reference Guide to Book Censorship in Schools and Public Libraries*(Westport: Greenwood Press, 2002). p. 136.

13. Linda Richards, "Judy Blume: On Censorship, Enjoying Life, and Staying in the Spotlight for 25 years," *January Magazine,* 1998, http://januarymagazine.com/profiles/blume.html.

14. Herbert N. Foerstel, *Banned in the U.S.A.: A Reference Guide to Book Censorship in Schools and Public Libraries*(Westport: Greenwood Press, 2002). p. 133.

15. Ibid., p. 134.

16. Linda Richards, "Judy Blume: On Censorship, Enjoying Life, and Staying in the Spotlight for 25 years," *January Magazine,* 1998, http://januarymagazine.com/profiles/blume.html.

17. Connie G. Rockman, ed., *Eighth Book of Junior Authors and Illustrators* (New York: H. W. Wilson, 2000).

18. NPR.org, "Talk of the Nation: Teens Across America," October 21, 1998, http://www.npr.org/templates/story/story.php?storyId=1009881.

19. New York Public Library (online), *Author Chat with Judy Blume,* November 19, 2002, http://teenlink.nypl.org/blume_txt.html.

20. Scholastic.com, "Authors & Books," Judy Blume (location on Web site), http://www2.scholastic.com/teachers/authorsandbooks/authorstudies/authorhome.jhtml.

21. Ibid.

22. Press material from Random House.

23. Ibid.

24. Carol Stocker, "Reading Judy Blume," *Boston Globe,* October 22, 1981, http://infoweb.newsbank.com/iw-search/we/InfoWeb?p_action=doc&p_docid=0EB9757462953297&p_docnum=8&p_queryname=2&p_product=NewsBank&p_theme=aggregated4&p_nbid=P5DL52JLMTE4MjExMTQ0My4yMjgyOTU6MTo4OnJhLTE5NDQ5.

25. Judy Blume, "Helping Kids Deal With Divorce," *The San Francisco Chronicle*, May 1, 1986, People Section, p. 27.

26. Ibid.

27. Carol Stocker, "Reading Judy Blume," *Boston Globe*, October 22, 1981, http://infoweb.newsbank.com/iw-search/we/InfoWeb?p_action=doc&p_docid=0EB9757462953297&p_docnum=8&p_queryname=2&p_product=NewsBank&p_theme=aggregated4&p_nbid=P5DL52JLMTE4MjExMTQ0My4yMjgyOTU6MTo4OnJhLTE5NDQ5.

28. Ibid.

29. Ibid.

30. Michelle Green, "After Two Divorces, Judy Blume Blossoms as an Unmarried Woman," *People Weekly*, March 19, 1984.

Chapter 4

HITTING HER STRIDE

Tales of a Fourth Grade Nothing was first written as a picture book early in Blume's career.[1] The story featured a fourth grader named Peter Hatcher whose irrepressible two-year-old brother, nicknamed Fudge, is constantly getting into mischief and embarrassing him. It was inspired by a newspaper article Judy's babysitter gave her about a toddler who had swallowed the family's small pet turtle. "There was a follow-up every day. Eventually there was a headline: 'Hooray! The Turtle Has Passed!'"[2]

She originally called the book *Peter, Fudge and Dribble* but it was rejected by all the publishers she submitted the manuscript to. After Judy had had several books published, her agent submitted the story to an editor at E. P. Dutton. The editor liked the story but suggested that Judy expand it into a full length book about the Hatcher family, keeping the turtle swallowing incident as one of the chapters.

"I loved her idea and went home fired up and ready to write," Judy says. "That summer I wrote the book, basing the character of Fudge on my son, Larry, when he was a toddler; a very interesting child. I hope he was never embarrassed. He did a lot of the things Fudge does, but he never swallowed a turtle."[3] Although a comedy, the book delicately addresses issues of sibling rivalry and the failure of parents to sometimes notice one of their children is feeling neglected. After Fudge swallows Dribble, Peter's tiny turtle, their parents are initially only concerned with making sure Fudge recovers, not with Peter's upset over the death of a loved pet. Although parents are not always redeemed in Blume's books, in this case the Hatchers get Peter a dog by way of apology for not being more sensitive to his feelings. Peter names the dog Turtle.

Judy believes that was the only time in her career before or since that a first draft was published "as is" without her having to revise it. "I was ecstatic."[4] The only change made was to the title.

Normally, Judy says, she does an average of five rewrites. "I'm a rewriter. It's my favorite part. The first draft is torture for me. The next draft is usually OK, and the next makes it even better."[5] But, she adds, "I never rewrite the dialogue."[6]

Tales of a Fourth Grade Nothing would eventually sell over six million copies and is the third-highest-selling children's trade paperback ever, trailing only *Charlotte's Web*, by E. B. White, and S. E. Hinton's *The Outsiders*. It would also be the first group of characters Blume felt compelled to revisit. Her next book, *Otherwise Known as Sheila the Great*, featured Peter Hatcher's nemesis, Sheila Tubman.

"Sheila has all of my childhood fears—dogs, swimming, thunderstorms, night terrors," Judy says. "It was said in my family that Judy is afraid of her own shadow. My older brother delighted in torturing me, taking advantage of my fears, jumping out of the shadows with a sheet over his head while making ghostly sounds. I can still be easily frightened but I'm proud to say I'm no longer afraid of dogs—most dogs, anyway—and I did learn to swim. As for thunderstorms . . . okay, I admit it, I'm phobic. If I'm home and it's a big boomer, I might seek refuge in my 'thunder' closet.

"Unlike me, Sheila covers her fears with bravado."[7]

It was a formula Blume would use throughout her career: blending the facts and experiences of her life within the fictional worlds she created in her books. At some point, everything, and everyone in Judy's life would end up in her writing. Her characters resonated because Blume was willing to completely expose herself through them—even when it hurt emotionally or showed her failings. With each book, Judy showed herself not to be just a prolific writer but a courageous one as well, unafraid to make herself vulnerable to her readers

"Those of us who grow up to write about young people do bring our own fears, as children, and worries, into it, try to make other kids feel OK,"[8] Blume agrees.

Writing honestly for children also meant being willing to ruffle feathers and to unblinkingly discuss topics that many adults shy away from, such as physical deformity.

The title character in *Deenie* is an attractive, self-assured seventh grader. Her sister is considered the family brain; Deenie the beauty. But the modeling career her mother envisions is derailed when Deenie is diagnosed with scoliosis, or curvature of the spine. Literally overnight, Deenie becomes seen as "disabled" because she has to wear a restrictive brace for four years to correct the condition. But the subtext is about how pigeon-holing or labeling children can adversely affect them.

Blume was inspired to write the book after meeting a fourteen-year-old girl with scoliosis. "She seemed to be adjusting well to her condition and her brace but her mother was in tears over the situation," Judy recalls, stressing that the family in *Deenie* is purely fictional. "I set the book in the town where I grew up and sent Deenie and her friends to my junior high school."[9]

Since Blume wrote the book, new treatments for the condition have been developed, but the impact of parental expectation remains as powerful now as it was thirty years ago.

Typically, *Deenie* is mostly remembered as being one of the most banned books of the twentieth century because of its frank discussion, and subtle depiction, of masturbation. Between her mother's frustration that Deenie won't be modeling any time soon and the embarrassment of walking around in a brace and suspecting the boy she has a crush on won't want to kiss her anymore, Deenie is stressed out.

She finds relief, and release, by "touching myself . . . my special place."[10] But she worries that anything that feels that good must be bad so she writes her gym teacher an anonymous note wanting to know. . .

> "Do normal people touch their bodies before they go to sleep and is it all right to do that?"
>
> After answering some menstruation-related questions girls have posed, the physical education teacher addresses Deenie's query. "Can anyone help us with an answer?'"
>
> After one girl answers that boys who do such things are in danger of going blind, developing acne, or physical deformities, Mrs. Rappoport responds: "I can see you've got a lot of misinformation. Does anyone here know the word for stimulating our genitals? Because that's what we're talking about, you know."
>
> It got very quiet in the gym. Nobody said anything for a long time. Then one girl spoke. "I think it's called masturbation."
>
> "That's right," Mrs. Rappoport told us. "And it's not a word you should be afraid of. . . . First of all, it's normal and harmless to masturbate."
>
> —*Deenie*

Not exactly hard-core pornography but it might as well have been for the uproar it caused.

"Masturbation is such a frightening idea to some adults they would rather ban a book than talk to their children about it. Sad for their kids,"[11] Blume observes. "You know, every kid wants to feel normal. Every kid wants to feel OK. . . . The little bits of masturbation in *Deenie*," Judy says, came directly from her own childhood experiences. "I knew I had a special place and I got a special feeling, but I was sure I was the only one. . . . If I could've read about it, I would've known: *Oh, there's a name for this. And it's a natural and normal thing to do*. And you don't really have to make bargains with God about doing it. It's OK, nothing bad's going to happen to you."[12]

Blume firmly believes masturbation is healthy, normal, and positive. "I don't think one ever needs to teach children to do it—they either do or they don't."[13]

There was also a gender bias toward *Deenie*. Blume recalls the time a school principal would not allow the librarian to offer the book because Deenie masturbated . . . but commented his decision would have been different if Deenie had been a boy. His implication being, masturbation was normal for boys but not normal for girls. Those kinds of comments only made Blume more determined to keep writing honest stories.

So just like in real life, her books didn't necessarily have "happy endings," just realistic ones. In *Blubber* an overweight girl, Linda, is mercilessly taunted and bullied by a group of girls led by Wendy. But most of the perpetrators don't get their comeuppance in the end. Life just goes on.

"When my daughter Randy was a fifth grader, she came home from school with stories about her classmates and how badly they were treating each other." Blume says her daughter was quiet and shy and not part of the popular group. "She was an observer. And she was especially upset by the way one girl in her class, Cindy, had become the victim of the class leader. . . .[14] I don't think my daughter felt brave enough to jump in and do anything about it. It's scary because you never know if someone will turn on you, and do that to you. That's why I think a lot of kids keep quiet."[15]

Nor does the bullied child come forward, too humiliated or afraid of retribution. But, Blume says, "I believe the best thing you can do if it happens to you is don't keep it a secret, because keeping it a secret makes it that much worse." She remembers the one child who wrote and told her, *The fear is sickening*. "So, don't keep that fear in. Talk to the people you trust most."[16]

In Cindy's case, most of the bullying took place during lunch or on the school bus, so the teacher was oblivious. "Her lack of awareness made it easy for the class leader to use her power in an evil way, victimizing one student and turning classmate against classmate. . . . Some adults are bothered by the language and the cruelty, but the kids get it. They live it. In some places the book is used in teacher training classes to help future teachers understand classroom dynamics.[17]

"What surprises me is how willing some kids are to reverse roles. The one who has been victimized will often, if given the chance, jump right in and participate in the victimization of someone else."[18]

> "Think how you would feel if it happened to you. Try to put yourself in her place."
> "I could never be in her place," Jill replies.
> "Don't be so sure," her mother says.
>
> —*Blubber*

Jill—who has been one of Linda's tormentors—eventually develops a conscience. That's when she becomes Wendy's next target. At the end of the book Jill finds herself just as ostracized as Linda, learning a harsh lesson on the consequences of standing up for one's beliefs.

Blume believes *Blubber* is the best book she's written for younger children. Critics, however, accused her of moral ambiguity.

"I now understand to mean that the bad guys go unpunished, or as the book banners put it, evil goes unpunished. In other words, I don't beat the kids over the head with the message."[19]

But Blume knows children learn at an early age that mean kids don't always get caught; bad guys sometimes win. To pretend otherwise would not only be dishonest but insulting to their intelligence and contrary to their experience. She can never understand when a parent says accusingly, "*You didn't tell them this was wrong. . . .* But, of course, kids are often much more able to deal with things."[20]

Blume admits that overall, her children—who were 14 and 12 respectively—dealt better with the emotional fallout of her divorce from John than she did. Judy had an advantage over most women of that era in that she was able to financially support herself through writing. "I like to think I would have been brave enough to change my life anyway, because it was a matter of survival and I was going down the drain."[21] Even so, "It was very, very, very traumatic," she recalls. "What I knew was how to be married."[22]

> So where did things go wrong, Norm? So what happened? It seemed all right then. Comfortable. Safe. We had our babies. We made a life together. But now I'm sick. There isn't any rash, no fever, but I'm sick inside. . . And I'm so fucking scared.

I wish a big bird would fly up to me, take me in its mouth and carry me off, dropping me far away . . . anywhere . . . but far from you.

—Wifey

Judy had been married sixteen years. "The next years were more stressful, more painful, more threatening than anything I have ever experienced. That we survived reasonably intact says a lot for the strength of family love, for the ability of children to cope and for how basically decent people can hurt each other terribly, come close to the breaking point, then pull themselves back together again."[23]

Before telling her husband and kids she wanted a divorce, Blume sought guidance from a counselor. "She said, *The children will ask you why—and you better have some answers.* It is much harder for children to understand why their parents are splitting up when there hasn't been any fighting, when either one or both parents have been keeping their feelings of unhappiness, resentment, disappointment and anger inside. It's hard to explain to your kids why this has become an intolerable situation for you. I don't think I was able to do a very good job of it then."[24]

All Judy knew for certain was that she was not happy. Her marriage lacked the emotional and physical intimacy she craved, making her "itchy" to get out there and live. Even though she needed to leave the marriage to find herself and the relationship that would complete her, making the break was devastating. "It was hard on all of us, more painful than I could have imagined, but somehow we muddled through and it wasn't the end of any of our worlds, though on some days it might have felt like it."[25]

To help her children—and herself—through it, they each wrote a letter about his or her feelings to the other. Then they read the letters privately and later had a group cry. "It's really hard to be a child and no one has shown just how hard it is," Blume observes. "No, I wouldn't be a kid again."[26]

Dear Kids: Remember, during and after a divorce, your parents are suffering too. That doesn't make it any easier, I know, but it's a fact. It's very hard in the beginning, especially if your parents are fighting and you feel caught in the middle, to keep your relationship with both parents going strong. It's OK for you to tell them you're not taking sides. . . . There may be times when you will have to remind your parents that this is their divorce, not yours. And that you still love both of them.

—Letters to Judy: What Kids Wish They Could Tell You

Not living under the same roof with John was an adjustment for both kids and father. "When John and I first split up, the kids would visit him on weekends. He took them to expensive restaurants and to see plays and movies. He entertained them lavishly, not to compete with me, but because he didn't know what else to do. He wanted to show them that he cared, that he loved them, and extravagant weekends were the only way he knew how to do that."[27]

But the pressure to constantly entertain his children burnt John out. He went from taking them everywhere to taking them nowhere. At first Randy and Larry were disappointed. "It took years to get it worked out so that they were comfortable together, so that they did not expect to be entertained non-stop when they were with him, and for him to see that it was OK to take them out sometimes, just because he felt like it."[28]

Judy had even more difficulty adjusting to life after John. "I didn't know how to be unmarried,"[29] she says. Instead of taking the time to learn, Judy impulsively jumped into a new relationship that would prove disastrous.

NOTES

1. "Judy Blume Looks Back," *People*, November 29, 2004, p. 59.

2. Sue Corbett, "Judy Blume Tackles Kids and Money in Her Hero's Latest Adventures," *The Miami Herald*, January 15, 2003, http://www.highbeam.com/doc/1G1–119242588.html.

3. Judy Blume, *Tales of a Fourth Grade Nothing*,(Dutton, 1972), http://www.judyblume.com/tales.html.

4. Ibid.

5. Judy Green, "Sense and Censorship," *The Sacramento Bee,* October 2, 2002, E1.

6. Richard Flaste, "Viewing Childhood as It Is," *New York Times,* September 29, 1976, http://select.nytimes.com/mem/archive/pdf?res=F40F1EFE3B58167493CBAB1782D85F428785F9.

7. Judy Blume, *Otherwise Known as Sheila the Great*, (New York: E. P. Dutton, 1972), http://www.judyblume.com/sheila.html.

8. NPR.org, "Talk of the Nation: Teens Across America," October 21, 1998, http://www.npr.org/templates/story/story.php?storyId=1009881.

9. Teens@Random.com, *Deenie*, (Bradbury, 1973), http://www.randomhouse.com/teens/catalog/display.pperl?isbn=9780440932598.

10. Kathryn Jean Lopez, "Early Blumers: In Defense of Censorship," *National Review Online*, Books on NRO Weekend, http://www.nationalreview.com/weekend/books/books-lopez093000.shtml (accessed October 1, 2000).

11. "Judy Blume Goes Hollywood (Finally)," *Plastic,* http://www.plastic.com/article.html;sid=04/04/09/14122366.x.

12. "Talk of the Nation: Teens Across America," October 21, NPR.org, 1998, http://www.npr.org/templates/story/story.php?storyId=1009881.

13. William Leith, "Teen Spirit," *The Independent (London)*. July 18, 1999, http://www.highbeam.com/doc/1P2–5001703.html.

14. Judy Blume, *Letters to Judy: What Your Kids Wish They Could Tell You* (New York: G. P. Putnam's Sons, 1986).

15. Random House.com, *Interview with Judy Blume*, http://www.randomhouse.com/teachers/catalog/display.pperl?isbn=9780440407072&view=rg.

16. Ibid.

17. Judy Blume, *Blubber*, (Bradbury, 1974), http://www.judyblume.com/blubber.html.

18. Judy Blume, *Letters to Judy: What Your Kids Wish They Could Tell You* (New York: G. P. Putnam's Sons, 1986).

19. Herbert N. Foerstel, *Banned in the U.S.A: A Reference Guide to Book Censorship in Schools and Public Libraries* (Westport: Greenwood Press, 2002), p. 136 (35).

20. Sandy Rovner, "Judy Blume: Talking It Out," *Washington Post*, November 3, 1981, B1.

21. Rebecca Ascher Walsh, "The Fudge Report," *Entertainment Weekly*, October 11, 2002, p.77.

22. Enid Nemy, "It's Judy Blume, New Yorker," *New York Times*, October 3, 1982, http://select.nytimes.com/search/restricted/article?res=F30711FB345C0C708CDDA90994DA484D81.

23. Judy Blume, *Letters to Judy: What Your Kids Wish They Could Tell You* (New York: G. P. Putnam's Sons, 1986).

24. Ibid.

25. *Meet the Writers*, Barnes & Noble.com, http://www.barnesandnoble.com/writers/writerdetails.asp?cid=883118.

26. Richard Flaste, "Viewing Childhood as It Is," *New York Times*, September 29, 1976, http://select.nytimes.com/mem/archive/pdf?res=F40F1EFE3B58167493CBAB1782D85F428785F9.

27. Judy Blume, *Letters to Judy: What Your Kids Wish They Could Tell You* (New York: G. P. Putnam's Sons, 1986).

28. Ibid.

29. Enid Nemy, "It's Judy Blume, New Yorker," *New York Times*, October 3, 1982, http://select.nytimes.com/search/restricted/article?res=F30711FB345C0C708CDDA90994DA484D81.

Chapter 5

IMPULSIVE

Being single left Judy unsettled. So just a year after divorcing John, she rushed recklessly into another marriage. "I was the classic story; someone who couldn't stand not being married,"[1] she admits. "So I jumped into the arms of the first man who came along and said, *Hello, how are you?* in a nice way. . . .[2] I chose more wisely at 21 than I did at 37."[3]

Thomas A. Kitchens was a physicist and after their wedding, Judy and her children moved with him to Los Alamos, New Mexico, home of the National Laboratory and where the atom bomb was developed during World War II. Judy later described Los Alamos as a "fearful town," and calls it "Stepford," an allusion to the movie in which housewives were turned into automatons so they would be the perfect wives.

It didn't take her long to realize she had made a mistake. She says her impulsive marriage and move to New Mexico traumatized them—and her. "It was a disaster; a total disaster. After a couple years, I got out."[4] But during those years with Kitchens, Blume says, "I cried every day. Anyone who thinks my life was cupcakes all the way is wrong."[5]

Blume found solace in her writing. Her next book, however, would be accompanied by a controversy that once again found the center of a morality firestorm. The idea for *Forever* actually came from Judy's then-fourteen-year-old daughter Randy. "She was reading a lot of books which were all about pregnancy and terrible things that happen because of sex,"[6] Blume recalls, where the girl always got pregnant and had a grisly abortion.

"Girls in these books had no sexual feelings and boys had no feelings other than sexual. Neither took responsibility for their actions,"[7] Blume recalls. "And she said, *Couldn't there ever be a book about two kids who do it and nobody has to die?*"[8]

Judy warmed to the idea immediately, saying she "hated the idea of sex and punishment"[9] always going hand-in-hand. "I wanted to present another kind of story; one in which two seniors in high school fall in love, decide together to have sex, and act responsibly. . . ."[10] I wanted to say one can be sexual and responsible."[11] But Blume maintains her purpose wasn't to challenge conservative morals but simply because her daughter asked her to.

At its heart, *Forever* is about first love. High school senior Katherine meets Michael on New Year's Eve and they begin a romance. As they fall in love, their physical attraction deepens and their relationship becomes more and more sexual. Michael has had sex before; Katherine is a virgin. Her decision to make love to Michael isn't impulsive; she has thought it over at length and truly believes the love she shares with Michael will last forever—something her friend Erica thinks is a bit overblown.

> Erica: It might not be a bad idea to get laid before college.
> Katherine: What about love?
> Erica: You don't need love to have sex.
> Katherine: But it means more that way.
> Erica: Oh, I don't know. . . . You're a romantic. . . . I'm a realist. . . .
> we look at sex differently. I see it as a physical thing and you see
> it as a way of expressing love.
>
> —*Forever*

After she starts dating Michael and it's clear he is her first serious love, Katherine's grandmother—a proud feminist who works with Planned Parenthood—sends her a pile of literature about birth control and venereal diseases. Katherine reads it all and also discusses it with her mother. By that time, she feels like an expert.

> When I'd finished I thought, well, I can start a service in school
> I know so much, which might not be a bad idea, considering
> there is a girl in my gym class who, until this year, never knew
> that intercourse was how you got pregnant, and she's already
> done it!
>
> —*Forever*

Once Katherine and Michael start having sex, she goes to a clinic to get birth control, in addition to the condoms Michael has been using.

Blume takes the opportunity to impart a lot of practical information about gynecological exams, female anatomy, self breast exams and the choices of birth control available. In recent editions of the book, there is a warning included that in addition to whatever birth control a young woman uses, a condom should also be used to prevent the spread of sexually transmitted diseases.

"The seventies were a time when sexual responsibility meant preventing unwanted pregnancy," Blume notes. "Today, sexual responsibility also means preventing sexually transmitted diseases, including HIV/AIDS. . . . If you're going to become sexually active, then you have to take responsibility for your own actions. So get the facts first."[12]

Making love brings Katherine and Michael closer emotionally and further convinces them their love is one that will last forever. But when summer comes, the couple is separated when Katherine is sent to camp and Michael takes a job out of state. In somewhat of a surprise twist, while at camp, Katherine finds herself attracted to another young man who is slightly older. When Michael comes back for a surprise visit, he's crushed when Katherine breaks off their relationship. He locks himself in the bathroom and repeatedly flushes the toilet so Katherine won't hear that he's crying.

Late author Norma Klein wrote that *Forever* "showed that boys are often as vulnerable and sensitive as girls when it comes to their first sexual experience. It showed that there are no rules about what will cause pleasure or pain; that each person, as he or she emerges into the adult world, must find a way to live and love that makes sense to him or her, even if that way is at odds with the beliefs of parents or community."[13]

Blume puts it more simply. "I'm a storyteller, that's all. I was saying not only can you fall in love, and that love might not last, but that if you're going to be sexual and have intercourse, you should be responsible. Also I was saying that boys get equally hurt . . . I have a son."[14]

Judy broke so many accepted literary conventions about teen sex that her publisher marketed *Forever* as Judy's first adult book, much to Blume's annoyance. No matter. Teenagers found it anyway. So did the author's critics.

"The young tend to follow the life-style of their peers," said G. Bott in *Junior Bookshelf*. "Will Katherine and Michael's affair help to impose yet another imprimatur on casual sex?"[15] David Rees wrote in *The Marble in the Water*, "What sort of picture would a being from another planet form of teenage and pre-teenage America were he able to read *Are You There, God? It's Me, Margaret* and *Forever*? He would imagine that youth was obsessed with bras, period pains, deodorants, orgasms, and family planning. . . . Adolescents do of course have period pains and worry about the size of their breasts or penises; they fall in love and some of them sleep together. There should obviously be a place for all these concerns in teenage novels," Rees agreed, but added that to write about them as much as Blume did "to the exclusion of everything else is doing youth a great disservice."[16]

An exasperated Blume denies *Forever* give teens carte blanche to have indiscriminate sex. "I've never had a letter from a kid saying, *I read Forever and then I went and did it*. They're saying, *I was really curious*, and they get caught up in the love story. In fact, I got a letter from an older girl who said if she'd read the book before, she might not have gone as far with her boyfriend . . . if she'd thought ahead."[17]

Judy defends her penchant for covering adolescent sexuality because, "it was uppermost in my mind when I was a kid: the need to know, and not knowing how to find out. . . . I write about what I know is true of kids going through those same stages. . . . My responsibility to be honest with my readers is my strongest motivation."[18]

While Judy fully intended for teens to read *Forever*, she was equally clear it was not intended for young children and should not be stacked in any library's children's section. Kids will ask her, "*How old do I have to be before I can read this book?*" Blume says, calling it an impossible question to answer. "I generally ask them to wait until they are at least 12 and hope that they have an adult to talk to about it when they are through. I like the idea of them reading it before they are sexually active, that is, if they can talk about it with an adult they can trust. . . ."[19] Some kids are ready at twelve, some not until later. They usually know themselves. If it makes them feel uncomfortable, they can put the book down. If they have questions it helps if they can ask an adult—who's also read the book—to answer them."[20]

In fact, Blume urges adults to read her books. "I hate to categorize books. I wish that older readers would read my books about young people, and I hope that younger readers will grow up to read what I have to say about adult life."[21]

What bothers Judy the most is the message she believes is being sent to kids by the efforts to restrict books like *Forever* and *Margaret*. "I feel terrible . . . because they're telling kids there are things we don't want you to know about and we don't want to talk to you about . . . but [these things] are healthy, natural and they're good."[22]

It's gotten back to the author that students have been told that if they choose one of her books for a school report, they will they will automatically have points taken off their grade. Oddly enough, Judy was equally uncomfortable learning some teachers read her book aloud to the class, believing reading was a personal experience

"I've always hoped that my books would be read the way I read books, which is to become involved in a story that I can't put down, to be swept away by a character, to be entertained and shown how other people live and solve their problems. All the reasons that I read fiction are the very reasons that I write fiction and hope what I write will be read. None of that involves the classroom."[23]

Given time, Blume got used to the idea of her books being integrated with classroom curriculum. "If handled sensitively, my books can be useful classroom tools. I know of one teacher who begins his course each year by reading *Blubber* aloud. . . . Of course, my *Fudge* books are probably the most commonly used in class because they are fun."[24]

Ironically, the controversy surrounding the book is probably what drew the attention of CBS television executives, who optioned the book in order to make a movie of the week out of it starring Stephanie Zimbalist as Katherine. "I was totally pleased with it," Blume said. "I didn't know any better. I thought it was great. They had a good director. They had a producer who really, really cared. And they had an executive producer who fought the network to be able to make it true to the book."[25]

Starring Sally J. Freedman As Herself was published in 1977. Blume says it's long been her dream to adapt the book into a stage musical. "I see the whole play, even hear the music, but I've got to find a way to translate what's in my head to paper," she explains. But even if *Sally J. Freedman: The Musical* never gets off the ground, Judy believes, "It's good to still have fantasies."[26]

In *Wifey* Sandy Pressman has all sorts of fantasies—the kind that make some people blush. Growing up, Sandy was raised to be a wife and mother, and to not expect much else. But after twelve years of marriage, she begins to think she's missing out on life. The summer her children go away to camp, Sandy begins to take stock of her life and to spread her wings—both emotionally and sexually.

> Wifey is tired of chicken on Wednesdays and sex on Saturdays. This morning a mysterious motorcyclist flashed and revealed himself to Wifey and brought her frustrations into rigid focus!
>
> —Promotional copy for *Wifey*

It was the first time Judy wrote a book specifically aimed at an adult audience and not everyone was happy about it. Some younger fans were worried it meant she was finished writing books for them. Some critics sniped that she had finally written a "real" book. "Some were angry that I hadn't used a pseudonym, others that I even had such thoughts!" Blume remembers. "Plus, I began to hear from old boyfriends—and those who wanted to be."[27]

Judy says she turned to adult literature, quite simply, "because I was, and am, an adult. I am a grown woman and I wanted to deal with the experiences of a grown woman." When asked if there was a particular individual who was the inspiration for Sandy in *Wifey*, Blume immediately says. "Yes. *Me!*"[28]

In all her book prior to *Wifey*, Blume had revealed the feelings, confusion, fears and anxieties she experienced as a child and adolescent. As her marriage to Thomas Kitchens came to a slow, agonizing death, Judy was compelled to address that particular time in her life. But she met considerable resistance, with people telling her that writing an adult book would ruin her career. Or that if she had to write it, to use a pseudonym. Then there were those who seemed almost angry that she would address such adult material in a sexually explicit way.

"*Keep doing what you're doing; keep doing what you're doing,* everyone said," Blume recalls. "But it doesn't work that way. It has to come from deep down inside and everything had changed within my own life. What I want is the freedom to write what I want to write. The freedom to write is as important as the freedom to read."[29]

Wifey was released in 1978, the same year Judy and Tom Kitchens divorced. For as emotionally wrenching as her split had been with John, the divorce from Kitchens came as "a real relief. Everything I've read says you have to have a mourning period after a divorce, but I didn't. My mourning took place when I was in the marriage."[30]

As the 1970s drew to a close, Judy was finally ready to live on her own as an independent, single woman. She found comfort in her children, who were now young adults, and found fulfillment in her writing. And after the American social and political environment took an abrupt shift to the right, Blume would find her calling.

NOTES

1. Peter Gorner, "The Giddy/Sad, Flighty/Solid Life of Judy Blume," *Chicago Tribune*, March 15, 1985, p. 1.

2. Herbert A Michelson, "Kids Tell Her Their Secrets," *The Sacramento Bee*, May 5, 1986, B03.

3. Peter Gorner, "The Giddy/Sad, Flighty/Solid Life of Judy Blume," *Chicago Tribune*, March 15, 1985, p. 1.

4. Ibid., p. 14.

5. Michelle Green, "After Two Divorces, Judy Blume Blossoms as an Unmarried Woman," *People Weekly*, March 19, 1984.

6. Ellen Barry, "Judy Blume for President," *The Boston Phoenix*, May 26, 1998, http://weeklywire.com/ww/05–26–98/boston_feature_1.html.

7. Judy Blume, *Forever*, (Bradbury, 1975), http://www.judyblume.com/forever.html.

8. Ellen Barry, "Judy Blume for President," *The Boston Phoenix*, May 26, 1998, http://weeklywire.com/ww/05–26–98/boston_feature_1.html.

9. Ibid., p. 7.

10. Judy Blume, *Forever*, (Bradbury, 1975), http://www.judyblume.com/forever.html (accessed July 13, 2007).

11. "Judy Blume Looks Back," *People*, November 29, 2004, p. 59.

12. Judy Blume, *Forever*, (Bradbury, 1975), http://www.judyblume.com/forever.html (accessed July 13, 2007).

13. Sharon R. Mazzarella and Norma Odom Pecora, *Growing Up Girls: Popular Culture and the Construction of Identity* (New York: Peter Lang, 1999), p. 46.

14. Peter Gorner, "The Giddy/Sad, Flighty/Solid Life of Judy Blume," *Chicago Tribune*, March 15, 1985, p. 1.

15. BookRrags.com, "*Authors and Artists for Young Adults* on Judy Blume," http://www.bookrags.com/biography/judy-blume-aya/ (accessed July 13, 2007).

16. Rees, David. "Blume, Judy (Sussman Kitchens) 1938–: Critical Essay," BookRags.com, http://www.bookrags.com/criticism/blume-judy-sussman-kitchens-1938_2/ (accessed July 13, 2007).

17. Peter Gorner, "The Giddy/Sad, Flighty/Solid Life of Judy Blume," *Chicago Tribune*, March 15, 1985, p. 1.

18. BookRrags.com, "*Authors and Artists for Young Adults* on Judy Blume," http://www.bookrags.com/biography/judy-blume-aya/ (accessed July 13, 2007).

19. "Literary Lightning Rod," *Newsweek*, May 18, 2007, http://www.msnbc.msn.com/id/18725395/site/newsweek/.

20. Judy Blume, *Forever*, (Bradbury, 1975), http://www.judyblume.com/forever.html.

21. "Judy (Sussman) Blume," *Major Authors and Illustrators for Children and Young Adults*, 2nd ed., 8 vols. (Farmington Hills, MI: Thomson Gale, 2002).

22. Jessica Mosby, "Booked for an Encore: Judy Blume Mulls Over Retirement," U-Wire.com., October 7, 2002, http://www.highbeam.com/doc/1P1–68543379.html.

23. Herbert N. Foerstel, *Banned in the U.S.A.: A Reference Guide to Book Censorship in Schools and Public Libraries* (Westport: Greenwood Press, 2002), p. 138.

24. Ibid.

25. Linda Richards, "Judy Blume: On Censorship, Enjoying Life, and Staying in the Spotlight for 25 Years," *January Magazine*, 1998 http://januarymagazine.com/profiles/blume.html.

26. Judy Blume, "What's Up: Judy Talks About Her Latest Doings," February 2004, www.judyblume.com/from-judy.html.

27. Judy Blume, *Wifey*, (New York: G. P. Putnam, 1978), http://www.judy blume.com/wifey.html.

28. "Author Profile: Judy Blume," teenreads.com, http://www.teenreads.com/authors/au-blume-judy.asp (accessed July 13, 2007).

29. Cynthia Roberts, "Judy Blume: No More Kids' Stuff," Chronicle-Telegram, October 20, 1978, http://www.newspaperarchive.com/PdfViewer.aspx?img=29965 503&firstvisit=true&src=search&currentResult=2&currentPage=0.

30. Michelle Green, "After Two Divorces, Judy Blume Blossoms as an Unmarried Woman," *People Weekly*, March 19, 1984.

Chapter 6

A NEW CHAPTER

All the notoriety Judy Blume received for her frank discussions of puberty and sexuality overshadowed the popularity of her books, especially those aimed at younger children. Ever since the publication of *Tales of the Fourth Grade Nothing*, young readers had been writing Judy asking when there would be another Fudge book. Her answer was always the same: when—and if—she ever got another idea for one.

That moment came when Blume was in the shower covered in soap with a head full of shampoo—what would happen if the Hatchers had a new baby? "The idea seemed so simple I couldn't believe it had taken seven years," she says. Rather than having it set in Manhattan, she had Fudge and his family living in suburban Princeton, New Jersey for a year. Not coincidentally, Judy and her children had lived for a short time in Princeton. "The thing about funny books is, they have to spill out spontaneously, or they don't work," Blume explains. "Unlike a novel, which can take me three years and up to twenty drafts, Fudge books either come or they don't. Maybe that's why I write so few of them."[1]

When asked where she gets her inspiration, Blume sounds superstitious. "It comes from everyone, but if I start to think about it, I get nervous and worry that one day it'll stop coming."[2]

In *Superfudge*, Fudge is a four-year-old and Peter a sixth grader. Their new baby sister is named Tootsie. If possible, Fudge is even more of a handful because now he's suffering from a serious case of sibling rivalry with Tootsie, resenting the time and love his parents are giving their now-youngest child. So Fudge regresses and starts acting like a baby, too. Even though it causes Peter all sorts of trouble, on one level he understands.

I know it's stupid, but just for a minute I wished I could be
Mom's baby again, too.

—*Superfudge*

In a 1982 nationwide poll by the American Library Association, *Superfudge* ranked first in favorite children's books. Two other Blume books
came in second and third, and a total of ten Blume books were included in
the top fifty. *Superfudge* became Judy's best-selling children's book, and one
she has special affection for. "I wish I could write a book about Fudge every
year . . . but the ideas are not there."[3] Much of its appeal is that the book's
humor is based in reality. As one reviewer wrote: "Blume understands the
real nature of children's purity, which is in fact not precisely what it has
been cracked up to be by some of our more wishful colleagues."[4]

Judy stresses her belief that it is important, and healthy, for parents to
laugh with their children "whatever it is—their bathroom humor, their
nonsense humor. . . . You wonder, where does all the humor go when
people grow up?" She has a theory that parents worry that if they share
humor with their kids, or laugh with them, "they're giving up some kind
of authority."[5]

By 1980 when *Superfudge* was released, Judy's life was back on solid
ground. She was over the misery of her second marriage—"It should never
have been so there was nothing to save"[6]—and her books were more popular than ever. She was also adjusting to her children growing up. Randy
had graduated from the Santa Fe Preparatory School and was attending
Wesleyan University and Larry, two years younger, would be graduating
from high school soon.

Although still close to her children, Blume admitted she used to talk
to them more. But as they had gotten older, Randy and Larry were more
private individuals. And that meant Judy became more careful about not
using them as models for book characters, the way she did when they were
younger. "It was a big thing in my life to be able to say that my children
are these individual human beings, and I've got to get rid of the expecta-
tions that seem to come almost automatically."[7]

1980 also brought Judy a new beau, George Cooper, then a law professor
at Columbia. They met when the divorced Cooper came to Santa Fe, where
Blume was living, in order to see his twelve-year-old daughter, Amanda. A
friend suggested five women George might consider going to dinner with
while in town. He showed the list to his daughter and when she saw Judy's
name, the young girl flipped out. Although Cooper now pleads the Fifth
Amendment, Blume says his response was, "Not that woman who writes
those books that you read over and over and over again!"[8]

Nonetheless, urged on by his daughter Copper asked Blume to dinner . . . and that was that. Although Judy was smitten, she had learned her lesson with Kitchens. There would be no impulsive marriage this time around. Although she and George were soon in a committed relationship, she would wait seven years before marrying a third time. But that impulsive streak she showed with her second marriage is an admitted part of her trusting personality. Judy says her son teases that "I meet someone and say, *This is a nice person, why not work with this person?*" Blume laughingly admits she was guilty of choosing husbands in a similar fashion. "I just lucked out with George."[9]

With George in her life, Judy had more on her mind than books. She recalls how he once said in the beginning of their romance that she would be the perfect mate, if she only knew how to sail a boat. So Judy promptly enrolled in a sailing camp, "where I was an absolute, total failure." She says after spending three hours a day "studying the physics of sailing," she still can only tell which way the wind is blowing "by which way my hair sticks out."[10]

HOLLYWOOD KNOCKS

Blume's literary success did not go unnoticed in Hollywood. In 1978, CBS had produced the TV movie version of *Forever*. Not long after, Judy was approached about writing an original screenplay. Enjoying a new challenge, Judy accepted. The story Judy came up with was emotionally dark: After a teenage girl's father is murdered, she must find a way to cope with his death and move on with her life.

But when she took her script back to the producer, it got a lukewarm reception. Blume was told they needed something more visual and suggested that instead of being killed during a robbery, she could make it more adventurous by having the father die while exploring a cave, thinking it would be good if the audience could see a shot of his lifeless legs dangling.

George met Judy at the airport when she got back home from the meeting. "I fell into his arms weeping and carrying on and saying, *I can't do this.*"[11] So she didn't. Instead she turned it into her next book, *Tiger Eyes*.

The book starts on the day Davey Wexler's father is buried. While she was out on a date, he was shot and killed during a robbery at the family's convenience store in Atlantic City, New Jersey. As the loss sinks in, Davey's mother slips into a depression and because they live above the store, she has to face daily the place where her husband was killed.

So she takes Davey and her seven-year-old brother Jason to Los Alamos, New Mexico. They move in with Uncle Walter and Aunt Bitsy. Walter is a physicist at a nuclear plant. Davey thinks of him as someone thinking up new ways to kill people. At first Davey is miserable. She misses Atlantic City, she misses her boyfriend, she misses her best friend and most of all she misses her father. She hurts so much she literally feels dead inside. Slowly, Davey confronts her sense of loss and her deep grief begins to subside. She is befriended by an older Hispanic boy named Wolf who helps Davey confront her feelings.

> Newspapers are very big on facts, I think. . . . But not on feelings. Nobody writes about how it feels when your father is murdered. . . . Each of us must confront our own fears, must come face to face with them. How we handle our fears will determine where we go with the rest of our lives.
>
> —*Tiger Eyes*

Although the impetus of the story is murder, Blume says *Tiger Eyes* isn't about violence; it's about loss, especially sudden loss, such as when Blume lost her father to a heart attack when she was twenty-one.

"I was with him," she recalls. "I still can't write this without choking up, remembering. Davey's feelings about her father's sudden death were based on mine, though I'm not sure I was aware of it while I was writing the book."[12]

But once she finished the book, Judy realized just how close to the bone *Tiger Eyes* hit and how much she was channeling the love she felt for her father through Davey's love for her father. And made her loss Davey's loss. "That anger when you say, *Don't be dead, Daddy. Please let it be a big mistake. I need you and I want you.*" Blume says a person never gets over that, but it's her theory "that you keep someone alive by not being afraid to talk about it."[13]

Judy admits that the years she spent in Los Alamos while married to Kitchens was not a happy time, calling it "my bad years." However, the experience opened her up to a world she had never known and helped inspire characters she might not have created otherwise. Both George and her son believe *Tiger Eyes* is Blume's best book. But it took her a while to work through her own negative feelings about Los Alamos. "It took me two drafts to get the hate out: hate of the government mentality, the fear everyone felt, the loathing, the prejudice."[14]

Even though *Forever* and *Tiger Eyes* were definitely meant for older teens, Blume says she thinks of her others as books for young readers, "or maybe it should be books *about* young readers."[15] But what seemed to be of more importance for *Tiger Eyes* wasn't its genre designation, but that it didn't contain any "objectionable" material. And for Judy, that was a point of contention. She remembers a confrontation with her favorite editor, the same one who had worked with her on *Are You There God? It's Me, Margaret*; *Then Again, Maybe I Won't*; *Deenie*; *Blubber*; and *Forever* and who had always been unconditionally supportive. The memory Judy says, still "pains me to tell it and it pains him to hear it."[16]

The story actually begins with the 1980 presidential election. After Ronald Reagan—and his religious right, conservative political and social agenda—was voted into office, Blume says the would-be censors came out in force and she had the following conversation with her editor:

> "We want this book to be read by as many young people as possible, don't we?"
>
> "Yes."
>
> "Well, then we don't want to make this a target for the censors, do we? Is it really necessary to include this one passage?"[17]

The passage in question was a scene meant to show that after months of being numb, not allowing herself to feel anything emotionally, Davey is finally emerging from her grief. She allows herself to literally feel again by masturbating. "I felt my face grow hot, my stomach clench," Blume says. The editor agreed the scene was psychologically sound and delicately handled. But he also believed it begged for unwanted controversy. "I got the message—if you leave in those lines, the censors will come after this book. Librarians and teachers won't buy it. Book clubs won't take it. Everyone is too scared. The political climate has changed."[18]

Judy equates the way a writer brings a character to life on the page with how an artist brings life to a canvas, "through a series of brush strokes, each detail adding to the others, until we see the essence of the person." Conflicted, Blume argued why the passage should remain in the book but eventually she caved, calling herself, "not strong enough or brave enough to defy the editor I trusted and respected. . . . I willed myself not to give in to the tears of frustration and disappointment I felt coming . . . I still remember how alone I felt at that moment." Blume says that although she agreed to remove the passage, "I have regretted it ever since."[19]

It was the last time she acquiesced. The next time her editor wanted changes it was over three curse words. Again, the argument was that if she left the words in it might result in fewer sales. "I thought about it long and hard, but I concluded that the characters would not be real with sanitized speech. The book was eventually published without change."[20]

It was just the first salvo of the political sea change that washed over the country in the early 1980s. Blume called the climate *chilling* for a writer and said at the time, "I am finding more editorial resistance today to language and sexuality in books for young people than I did when I began to publish. . . . This climate of fear is contagious and dangerous."[21]

She struggled not to get discouraged or to start second-guessing herself. She realized that allowing her work to be abridged was "playing into the hands of the censors. I knew then it was all over for me unless I took a stand." So she began speaking out about her experiences. "And once I did, I found that I wasn't as alone as I'd thought."[22]

Good thing, too, because Blume's books were under increasing scrutiny. In early 1980, a parent named Bonnie Fogel of Bethesda, Maryland, complained to Montgomery County school officials after learning that a character in *Blubber* uses the word *bitch*. So in mid-February 1980, the book was taken off public school library shelves . . . six years after it was published. Schools in nearby Prince George County refused to purchase *Blubber* after a review committee determined it was cruel toward fat people. "We didn't feel it was the kind of material children should have without some supervision," a spokesman for the County School Superintendent said in a press release.[23]

Blume was one of several authors being targeted. What each book had in common was an unflinching realism. They were not fantasy books but reflections of the struggle adolescents go through. There are no fairy tale endings and parents aren't always wise and loving. And sex is a fact of life—and interest.

But the issue with *Blubber* was the raw depiction of bullying. That bullying was, and remains, a critical problem in almost every school in the country seemed beside the point to Blume critics. They were too offended by its presentation in the novel—the wrongdoers largely get away with their taunting—to address the actual issue of cruelty between children.

"What's really shocking," Fogel said, "is that there is no moral tone to the book. There's no adult or another child at the end who says, *This is wrong. This cruelty to others shouldn't be.*"

Blume patiently explains that was *exactly* the point—the fact that it's not resolved is the most important part of the book, in her opinion. "I don't think you can change children's behavior. You can make them aware." Judy agrees *Blubber* is hard-hitting but thinks, "Kids are awfully rough on each other. I'd rather get it out in the open than pretend it isn't there."[24]

In *Reading for the Love of It,* Michele Landsberg decried such stark realism. "When you think back to your childhood reading, what was it that stirred, excited, thrilled you with the unfolding potential drama of life?" She lists fanciful characters such Mowgli, Tarzan, and Alice with her looking glass. "Or was it *a kid just like you,* worrying about gas pains, tomorrow's math test and Mom's pap smear?"[25]

Writer Mark Oppenheimer noted, "I know what the answer is supposed to be, but I confess that I choose Blume's realism. Has anyone wondered why Harper Lee, J. D. Salinger and S. E. Hinton all continue to be enormously popular, decade after decade, even as their novels become dated and children become ever more centered on our music-video present? It is because their novels are that rarest of species—realism for young people."[26]

And young people respond to it. "You should see the letters I get from kids," says Blume, who at times receives more than one thousand a month, "deeply personal letters about their feelings. They tell me, *I don't have anybody to talk to and I feel from your books that I can talk to you.*"[27]

Interestingly, the majority of her readers still write letters sent via snail mail as opposed to e-mail. On one hand, Blume says she loves e-mail. "I love the immediacy of it. But," she admits, "I do think it tends to be less personal. It doesn't feel as private as sitting down with paper and pencil and baring your soul. I've had many fewer e-mails about really serious issues in kids' lives," although Judy says she has had some "very seriously troubled kids contact me via e-mail."[28]

Blume considers herself lucky that young people identify with her characters. "First experiences, whether a first kiss, first period, first wet dream, first sexual relationship . . . these are the moments we never forget." Judy proudly admits she writes about the real world, "About families, friends, school, about changing bodies and changing relationships. These are still the most important things in my life, too."[29]

It's precisely because she writes about universal concerns that Blume never thinks of her work as groundbreaking. But she is aware that now everyone shares her personal attitudes about some subjects, such as sex. She comments that in *Forever,* "I was just telling a story about two seniors in high school who fall in love and decide to have sex." She wryly notes that if there was anything particularly groundbreaking about the books, it was that the two teens are sexually responsible. "Or maybe it's that Katherine enjoys her sexuality. There are still people who are bothered by that today."[30]

But for every Bonnie Fogel who believed Blume was inciting kids to behave badly, there were numerous others who recognized her importance to so many young readers. At the same time Fogel was protesting *Blubber*, the area's public library system purchased over one hundred copies of it. Ann Friedman, who oversaw choosing children's books, wasn't a fan of Blume's writing from a stylistic point of view but acknowledged "we have an obligation to be responsive to what kids are reading. . . . I have great faith that kids will figure out what's the right thing to do without having a moral lesson spelled out."[31]

Not everyone shared her faith.

NOTES

1. Judy Blume, *SuperFudge*, (New York: Dutton, 1980), http://www.judy blume.com/superfudge.html.

2. "Ask Them Yourself," *Family Weekly*, http://www.newspaperarchive.com/ PdfViewer.aspx?img=47394592 (accessed July 13, 2007).

3. "Judy (Sussman) Blume," *Dictionary of Literary Biography*, http://www. bookrags.com/biography/judy-sussman-blume-dlb/ (accessed July 13, 2007).

4. Ibid.

5. Sandy Rovner, "Judy Blume: Talking It Out," *The Washington Post*, November 3, 1981, B1.

6. Judy Blume, "Are You There, Reader? It's Me, Judy," *Chicago Sun-Times*, July 5, 1998, http://www.highbeam.com/doc/1P2–4455974.html.

7. Julie Salamon, "Young Audience Grows Up," *New York Times*, April 8, 2004, E1.

8. Jennifer Frey, "Fiction Heroine," *Washington Post*, November 17, 2004, C1.

9. Julie Salamon, "Girls' Pal Breaks into the Movies," *International Herald Tribune*, April 10, 2004, http://www.highbeam.com/doc/1P1–93345972.html.

10. Joseph P. Kahn, "Judy Blume's Summer Camp," *Boston Globe*, July 6, 1995, Living Section, p. 61.

11. Julie Salamon, "Young Audience Grows Up," *New York Times*, April 8, 2004, E1.

12. Judy Blume, *Tiger Eyes*, http://www.judyblume.com/tiger.html.

13. Sandy Rovner, "Judy Blume: Talking It Out," *Washington Post*, November 3, 1981, B1.

14. Carol Stocker, "Reading Judy Blume," *Boston Globe*, October 22, 1981, http://infoweb.newsbank.com/iw-search/we/InfoWeb?p_action=doc&p_ docid=0EB9757462953297&p_docnum=8&p_queryname=2&p_product= NewsBank&p_theme=aggregated4&p_nbid=P5DL52JLMTE4MjExMTQ0 My4yMjgyOTU6MTo4OnJhLTE5NDQ5.

15. Judy Blume, "Are You There, Reader? It's Me, Judy," *Chicago Sun-Times*, July 5, 1998, http://www.highbeam.com/doc/1P2–4455974.html.

16. Herbert N. Foerstel, *Banned in the U.S.A.: A Reference Guide to Book Censorship in Schools and Public Libraries* (Westport: Greenwood Press, 2002), p. 136.

17. Ibid., p. 137.

18. Judy Blume, ed., "Introduction" to *Places I Never Meant To Be* (New York: Simon & Shuster, 1999).

19. Ibid.

20. Ibid.

21. Norma Klein, "Some Thoughts on Censorship: An Author Symposium," *Top of the News*, Winter, 1983, EJ276815.

22. Judy Blume, ed., "Introduction," to *Places I Never Meant To Be*, New York: Simon & Shuster, 1999.

23. Lawrence Feinberg, "Schools' Use Of Candid Novels Draws Parents' Fire," *Washington Post*, February 25, 1980, A1.

24. Ibid.

25. Michele Landsberg, *Reading for the Love of It* (New York: Prentice Hall Press, 1987).

26. Mark Oppenheimer, "Why Judy Blume Endures," *New York Times Book Review*, November 16, 1997, http://www.judyblume.com/articles/oppenheimer.html.

27. Lawrence Feinberg, "Schools' Use Of Candid Novels Draws Parents' Fire," *Washington Post*, February 25, 1980, A1.

28. "I Love Email," August–Sept 2002, http://www.cynthialeitichsmith.com/auth-illJudyBlume.html (accessed July 13, 2007).

29. Amy Bryant, "teenwire.com Talks with Judy Blume," May 22, 2007, http://www.teenwire.com/infocus/2007/if-20070522p487-blume.php. Used with Permission from Planned Parenthood Federation of America, Inc.

30. Ibid.

31. Lawrence Feinberg, "Schools' Use of Candid Novels Draws Parents' Fire," *Washington Post*, February 25, 1980, A1.

Chapter 7

A CHANGING ENVIRONMENT

After living in New Mexico for five years, Judy was ready to go back home to the east coast. So when her son Larry graduated from Santa Fe Prep in 1981, she convinced George to leave the wide open spaces of the southwest for the mass of humanity that is New York. Blume got an apartment in Manhattan and felt energized being in the city again, joking at the time that people probably thought she was a crazy street lady because she found herself constantly singing as she walked down the street.

Blume and Cooper lived quietly, much more likely to be found in their favorite neighborhood eateries than in five-star restaurants. Judy also indulged in a long-held passion—dancing. She had taken lessons as a kid and when she returned to New York she signed up for tap lessons. Never one to do anything half-heartedly, she took class five days a week at a professional studio. She was so happy and her life with Cooper so fulfilling, it seemed she had less time—or perhaps drive—to write.

Her next published book was not exactly a book *she* wrote. The *Judy Blume Diary: The Place to Put Your Own Feelings* was a journal intended to encourage young people to write down their thoughts. The diary also included words of wisdom from Blume, selected quotes from her books, and an address book.

To some observers this seemed like crass commercialism—especially since Blume had always rigorously protected her books by limiting merchandizing. In other words, no one saw *Blubber* lunch boxes, nightshirts with a *Forever* log on it, or Judy Blume bras. The author bristled at the notion she was turning into a brand, or product. But she admitted people had tried, recalling "tacky stuff" like a Judy Blume board game where if you picked a card that says *Parents Divorcing* you get pushed back but if you pick the *You Started Your Period* card, you get to move forward. "People," Blume says wryly, "will cash in on anything."[1]

The reason Judy endorsed the *Diary* is because all the proceeds from sales financed and supported Blume's KIDS Fund (Knowledge, Independence, Decision-making and Sensitivity). The organization helps community groups that work with kids such as education programs for teenage mothers or workshops for kids whose parents are divorcing. "I don't think I write [just] about problems," she says. "I think I'm writing from something deeper."[2]

Blume says that when she was growing up, nobody in school encouraged her or her peers to write. As a teenager, though, she did keep a diary, which she "never would have shared it with anyone," and thinks it's very good practice to write feelings and thoughts down. But, she acknowledges, keeping a journal "is easier for some people than others."[3]

It would be two years before Judy's next book, *Smart Women*, was published in 1983. Like *Wifey*, this was intended for adults. While not autobiographical per se, Judy's life experiences very much inform the characters. B.B. and Margo are best friends with a lot in common. They are both divorced and have teenage daughters. They are successful: Margo is an architect and B.B. is a top real estate agent in Boulder, Colorado, where they live. They are friends with another divorcée, Clare. And when Margo falls in love with B.B.'s ex, they share a man, so to speak.

Blume says that while the story comes from real life, it's not necessarily *her* life. But she wanted to explore the question of what could happen if a forty-year-old woman falls in love again. She acknowledges that in most of her books, she identifies with one of the characters. But in *Smart Women*, she identified with four.

The book is about second chances. Blume admits that after her second divorce she was resigned to the possibility she might not have another serious romance. "I was a divorced woman with two teenagers, thankful for a good career, but convinced I would never find a lasting love relationship."[4]

> How come smart women like us keep falling in love with schmucks? . . . How could you respond in bed to someone you wanted to smash with a baseball bat?
>
> —*Smart Women*

And then, she says, "Bam! It hit me all over again. Of course, when you fall in love this time around, you bring all that baggage with you, not to mention your kids, who might not think it's all as romantic as you do," she acknowledges, adding that she thinks the teen characters in *Smart Women* are two of the best she'd ever written. "What teenager wants to know anything about mom or dad's sex life? And just when they're beginning to discover sex themselves!"[5]

Even though the book was classified as adult, her basic philosophy about writing remained the same as it was when writing for kids. Blume likes to think that she writes for everybody. "I think that my appeal has to do with feelings and with character identification," things that remain constant generation after generation. "That's what I really know."[6]

One point she wanted to explore was how children cope with a parent's new love interest. Another was to show that even a thoughtful, intelligent, caring person can make bad choices in romance that end up putting them and their children in unhealthy situations. "I love family life," she says. "I love kids. I think divorce is a tragedy, traumatic and horribly painful for everybody." She wrote *Smart Women* so parents might "think about what life is like for their kids."[7]

OUT OF THE NEST

With her career firmly established and George Cooper by her side, Blume's life was better than good. Even though she still resisted another walk down the matrimonial aisle, she frequently commented that she never felt more married. Judy had finally found her soul mate.

Her children were her pride and joy—and as independent as their mom. Larry was in college with an eye toward working in the entertainment industry and Randy was at Wesleyan University, planning to go to law school—until one of her friends mentioned he had recently taken flying lessons and was now soloing.

Randy had grown up fascinated with airplanes and says the part of family vacations she remembered most vividly was the flights. The friend's comment stirred something and Randy took a lesson at nearby Brainard Field in Hartford, Connecticut. That lesson led to others.

"I became totally obsessed," Randy recalls. "I read flying magazines tucked inside textbooks. I wrote all my papers about flying. And I knew that I wanted to be an airline pilot."[8]

By the time she graduated in 1983 Randy had earned her private pilot's license. She spent the summer at Judy's vacation home on Martha's Vineyard. But instead of preparing for law school, Randy was constantly reading flying magazines. Judy assumed it was just a passionate hobby and didn't nag at her to pay more attention to getting ready for law school.

Randy says the moment her mother said, "If that's what you want to do," she made her decision. "That was all the permission I needed."[9]

When she finally told her mother she wanted to defer graduate school to become a professional pilot, Judy Blume, the fantasy mother for millions of young readers, lost it. (Just the way any parent would.) Randy recalls her mother wailing, "How could this have happened? I've sent you to the best schools. I took you to museums, concerts, the theater. I kept the house filled with books. I didn't let you watch TV or eat Twinkies. Where did I go wrong?"[10]

The knee-jerk reaction was short-lived. Randy picked a flying school, approved by Judy. She eventually worked her way up and became a pilot for Continental Airlines, but quit once she wanted to start a family.

While corporate America was becoming more free thinking and inclusive, with women like Randy entering fields traditionally male, certain segments of the population were trying to dictate personal morality for the majority. If they found a book or a film or a television show objectionable, it wasn't enough for them to reject it. They wanted to deprive *everybody* access to the material, or take away the freedom of anonymously reading whatever one chose. Even though our Constitution specifically mandates separation of church and state, many of these decisions and efforts at censorship were based directly on religious beliefs.

It's a curiously American trait that we ignore attacks on civil liberties in general until it affects us directly. While the majority of Americans believe that parents have a right to oversee what their children read, many would take exception to one parent dictating another parent's choices. Still, few were vocally up in arms at the increasing number of incidents where books were removed from shelves because a minority objected to them, mostly because it was something happening "over there" in a different community from their own.

> Censorship: official restriction of any expression believed to threaten the political, social, or moral order.
>
> —*The Concise Columbia Encyclopedia*

In September 1983, in honor of Banned Book Week, the county libraries in the Washington, D.C., area presented a display of books that had been banned, beginning back in 387 B.C. when the Greeks tried to censor Homer, who is credited with authoring *The Iliad* and *The Odyssey*. In 1929, *Tarzan* was removed from the Los Angeles library because the King of the Jungle was "living in sin" with Jane. In 1983, two schools in Alabama banned *Doris Day: Her Own Story* because of "shocking" revelations about her troubled marriages and because the book wasn't in keeping with her "All-American image." Lewis Carroll's "Alice in Wonderland" was banned in China because the animal characters used human language and it was considered wrong to put animals and humans on the same level.

The point is, if we removed every book someone had an issue with, soon we'd have no books in any library.

Banned Book Week was established in 1982 by the American Library Association, or ALA. A spokesman for the ALA says the idea behind Banned Book Week was to "alert people that censorship has occurred in the past and is occurring today."[11] The ALA estimated that around seventy-five percent of all censorship efforts took place in schools.

Conservative activist Kris McGough called Banned Books Week unhelpful. "All it's doing is pitting parent against parent, parent against educator."

But the week also spotlighted the increasing efforts to censor reading material. Frequently, Judy Blume was the author being banned. In late 1984, three of her books—*Deenie, Then Again Maybe I Won't,* and *Blubber*—were banned from elementary school libraries in Peoria, Illinois. Officials said the books were pulled because libraries in elementary schools service grades kindergarten through eighth and Blume's books were not appropriate for students in the sixth grade and younger.

In a *Chicago Tribune* Voice of the People letter, one reader vented over Blume, calling her immature. "She proves what happens when an adolescent does not have the moral guidance to learn how to control or discipline one's self and therefore never matures out of self-centered temptations of adolescence.

"That she is a popular author and recommended by so many teachers and librarians who select reading lists makes me wonder about the maturity of the ones in those positions of authority."[12]

When news of the books' banning became public, a group of eight children's authors sent a letter appealing to Peoria's Board of Education to put the books back in the library. The authors said banning would "'teach a poor lesson, one of intolerance, distrust and of contempt" for the First Amendment which, they stated, protected not only "the freedoms to write, publish and read but also the freedom to decide what to read."[13]

One of the eight authors, Natalie Babbitt (*Tuck Everlasting*), noted, "Some parents and librarians have come down hard on Judy Blume for the occasional vulgarities in her stories." But those same vulgarities happen in real life, too, and "are presented in her books with honesty and full acceptance."[14]

Judith M. Goldberger (*The Looking Glass Factor*) found it ironic that "concerned parents and critics read Judy Blume out of context, and label the books while children and young adults read the whole books to find out what they are really about and to hear another voice talking about a host of matters with which they are concerned in their daily lives. The grownups, it seems, are the ones who read for the 'good' parts, more so than the children."[15]

Blume is troubled by the notion that books are banned to protect children. "They live in the same world we do. They see things and hear things." She thinks it's more harmful to prevent them from getting information "because what they imagine, and have to deal with alone, is usually scarier than the truth. Sexuality and death—those are the two big secrets we try to keep from children, partly because the adult world isn't comfortable with them either. But it certainly hasn't kept kids from being frightened of those things."[16]

Blume also worries that some authors use sex simply as a selling point for their books, exploiting it rather than helping kids understand it. "I don't believe that sex is why kids like my books. The impression I get, from letter after letter, is that a great many kids don't communicate with their parents. They feel alone in the world. Sometimes, reading books that deal with other kids who feel the same things they do, it makes them feel less alone."[17]

Despite her strong opinions on book banning and censorship, Blume did not ever actively defend her books. "I frankly feel that my job is to write the books, not to defend them," she explains. "It is always the reader's job to defend the books, to ensure that they are available."[18] Such as the seventh grade girl who spoke before the school board in defense of *Deenie*. She explained that the book had helped her explain her own scoliosis to her friends and that she needed someone to explain what in the book was bad. "Such comments are far more persuasive and more important than anything Judy Blume could say before a school board,"[19] Blume says.

In December, 1984, Peoria's public school trustees voted 5–2 to return the three Blume titles back to the library. The books would be restricted to older readers or to any student with parental consent. But it was just one small victory in an ongoing battle. A 1985 study conducted by the Washington, D.C.–based People for the American Way noted a nearly 40 percent increase from 1984 of censorship incidents.

"This year, we are seeing a concerted effort to rid the schools of everything but the three R's," said Barbara Parker, then-education policy director of PfAW. "Public education as anything beyond rote memorization of facts has become controversial."[20]

The report showed that every publisher of high school literature anthologies had deleted 400 lines from *Romeo & Juliet* to "de-romanticize" Shakespeare's masterpiece. Legislation passed after Ronald Reagan's election in 1980 gave schools broader leeway to remove "objectionable" material, so among the books most frequently targeted were *The Diary of Anne Frank*, Robert Cormier's *The Chocolate War*, John Steinbeck's *Of Mice and Men*, J. D. Salinger's *The Catcher in the Rye*, and Blume's *Deenie, Blubber, Tiger Eyes*, and *Then Again Maybe I Won't*.

According to the PfAW report, most of the complaints came from Jerry Falwell's Moral Majority and the national Pro-Family Forum, which PfAW called a "major assault (by right-wing organizations) on school curriculum and counseling programs."[21]

Obviously, both sides of the political spectrum have used censorship. Liberal groups have protested both *To Kill a Mockingbird* and *The Adventures of Huckleberry Finn* because of perceived racism. But the majority of efforts to ban books come from conservative groups, according to PfAW, the ALA, and the American Booksellers Association.

Blume thinks the most destructive thing about censorship is that writers just starting out will censor themselves, thinking, "I can't write about that; I can't put it that way; I can't get inside this character and let this character speak in his or her real voice," because they'll be too worried publishers will think it too controversial and it won't get sold. "I do worry about that."[22]

Certain parts of the country had more instances of book bannings than others. The American south in the 1980s was one of the busiest.

Outside of Atlanta in 1985, *Deenie* was the center of a passionate censorship battle. On one side was the Concerned Citizens of Gwinnett, founded by Mrs. Theresa Wilson after her daughter brought the book home. When Mrs. Wilson discovered the book discusses masturbation, she set out to get the book removed from the school library.

On the other side was Free Speech Movement of Gwinnett, which asked Georgia's board of education to order the county school board to reinstate *Deenie*. The movement's leader, George Wilson (no relation to Theresa Wilson) said, "No one is obligated to read this book, but I want my child to have the option to go into the school library and pick out any book she wants, without someone else's parent dictating what she can read."[23] Both George and his daughter read the book.

The fight had implications beyond Blume's work. Theresa Wilson made it clear she intended to get other books, including textbooks, banned, and sought help from the Freedom Foundation and the Moral Majority. "I'm hearing about all kinds of other books in our schools that I'd object to, and now I wonder what good did it do just to get rid of *Deenie*."[24]

The books, and textbooks, she took issue with were any that "sympathize with communism, encourage premarital sex or experimenting with drugs, take pro-abortion positions and stress evolution without teaching creationism, too."[25] (The American Civil Liberties Union reported in 1985 that twenty-four of Alabama's 130 school districts used textbooks that did not mention evolution.) She later targeted *Confessions of an Only Child* by Norma Klein. Her objection to the book is that a character swears using God's name in vain.

George Wilson admitted he had never been involved as an activist before but "I think there is something sacred about a library," he said. "Ideas don't scare me. The absence of ideas scares me."[26]

Mrs. Wilson saw nothing wrong with censoring books when it came to children. "This kind of censorship has increased because parents are more concerned about schools taking away our authority with our children."[27]

Ironically, as soon as it was announced that the Concerned Citizens of Gwinnett were successful in getting *Deenie* out of general circulation and restricted, most bookstores in the area immediately sold out of *Deenie*. And in the county library system, all sixteen copies had been checked out, with waiting lists on them all.

Blume admits that if someone told her when she began to write that she would end up one of the most banned writers in America, "I'd have laughed." Her publishers did not always inform Judy of the complaints against her books. "They believed if I didn't know . . . I wouldn't be intimidated."[28]

Some stories still filtered their way back to Blume but in the beginning she wasn't concerned. "There was no organized effort to ban my books. . . . The seventies were a good decade for writers and readers. Many of us came of age during those years, writing from our hearts and guts, finding editors and publishers who believed in us, who willingly took risks to help us find our audience. We were free to write about real kids in the real world. Kids with feelings and emotions, kids with real families, kids like we once were."[29]

Blume says that atmosphere of creative freedom came to an abrupt halt after Reagan took office. She said the censors became organized and determined. "Not only would they decide what their children could read but what all children could read. It was the beginning of the decade that wouldn't go away, that still won't go away."[30]

NOTES

1. Sandy Rovner, "Judy Blume: Talking It Out," *Washington Post*, November 3, 1981, B1.

2. Randy Sue Coburn, "A Best-Selling but Much-Censored Author," *San Francisco Chronicle*, August 12, 1985, p. 15.

3. "Author Chat with Judy Blume," November 19, 2002, http://teenlink. nypl.org/blume_txt.html.

4. Judy Blume, *Smart Women*, (New York: Putnam, 1983), http://www.judy blume.com/smart_women.html.

5. Ibid.

6. "Judy (Sussman) Blume," *Major Authors and Illustrators for Children and Young Adults*, 2nd ed., 8 vols. (Farmington Hills, MI: Thomson Gale, 2002).

7. Ibid.

8. Michael Kenney, "Air Apparent Randy Blume Talks about Her Love of Flying, Her First Novel, and Her Mother, Judy, Who Prefers Land," *Boston Globe*, May 25, 1999, E1.

9. Ibid.

10. Ibid.

11. Tom Vesey, "Banned Books On Display at County Libraries," *The Washington Post*, September 9, 1983, B1.

12. Kathryn Anderson, "No Blume Fan," *Chicago Tribune*, March 30, 1985, Perspective Section, p. 8.

13. "8 Who Write Children's Books Protest Ban on Blume Works," *New York Times*, November 20, 1984, http://query.nytimes.com/gst/fullpage.html?res=9904 E6D91F39F933A15752C1A962948260.

14. "Judy (Sussman) Blume," *Major Authors and Illustrators for Children and Young Adults*, 2nd ed., 8 vols. (Farmington Hills, MI: Thomson Gale, 2002).

15. Ibid.

16. Joyce Maynard, "Coming of Age with Judy Blume," *New York Times*, December 3, 1978, http://www.nytimes.com/books/98/09/13/specials/maynard-blume. html.

17. "Judy (Sussman) Blume," *Major Authors and Illustrators for Children and Young Adults*, 2nd ed., 8 vols.(Farmington Hills, MI: Thomson Gale, 2002).

18. Herbert N. Foerstel, *Banned in the U.S.A.: A Reference Guide to Book Censorship in Schools and Public Libraries* (Westport: Greenwood Press, 2002), p. 139.

19. Ibid.

20. "Censors Busy In the Schools," *The San Francisco Chronicle*, August 16, 1985, pg. 49.

21. Peter Schrag, "Censors In the Schools," *Sacramento Bee*, September 11, 1985, B6.

22. "Teens Across America," *Talk of the Nation*, NPR.org, October 21, 1998, http://www.npr.org/templates/story/story.php?storyId=1009881.

23. Michael Hirsley, "Book Banners, Free Speechers Square Off," *Chicago Tribune*, October 8, 1985, 13.

24. Ibid.

25. Ibid.

26. Ibid.

27. Michael Hirsley, "ACLU Senses an Upturn in School-book Censorship in South," *Chicago Tribune*, December 29, 1985, 6.

28. Judy Blume, ed. *Places I Never Meant to Be*, (New York: Simon & Shuster, 1999), http://www.judyblume.com/articles/places-intro.html.

29. Ibid.

30. Ibid.

Author Judy Blume poses in her New York apartment on May 1, 1998. AP Photo/ Suzanne Plunkett

Judy Blume arrives at the Glamour Magazine 2004 "Women of the Year" awards at the American Museum of Natural History on November 8, 2004 in New York City. AP Photo/Jennifer Graylock

Judy Blume signs copies of her books during a book-signing event in New York, Tuesday November 16, 2004. AP Photo/Bebeto Matthews

Judy Blume speaks after receiving the 2004 National Book Foundation Medal for distinguished contribution to American letters, at the 55th National Book Awards held in New York City, Wednesday, November 17, 2004. AP Photo/Stuart Ramson

Chapter 8

REACHING OUT TO YOUNG READERS

In the ten years between 1969 and 1979 Blume wrote fourteen books. But after meeting George Cooper, her prolificacy cooled. While she still had stories to tell, Judy had a personal life to which she also wanted to devote time. In 1984, *The Pain and the Great One* was released. Blume had originally written it in 1974 as a poem that appeared in *Free to be You and Me*. Now it was reworked as an illustrated story featuring an eight-year-old girl and a six-year-old boy who talk about each other and whom their parents love more.

"One rainy afternoon, when my children were about six and eight, and the house was filled with their friends, I suddenly got an idea," recalls Blume. "I sat right down and wrote this story. The cat is our first family pet."[1]

Blume says the characters are based on Randy and Larry, who used to call each other The Pain and The Great One when they were young. It's the favorite thing she's ever written for younger children.

"I love picture books," she says. "I think some of the best people in children's books are the ones who create their own picture books. I wish I could say I'm one of them, but I'm not."[2]

Although Blume was producing fewer books, it was the books she had already written—and the ongoing efforts to ban them—that kept her very much in the news. In the mid-1980s, the censorship battle was increasingly waged in the courts. In July, 1985, a new amendment to an existing Virginia state law went into effect that banned the display of any "sexually explicit" material "for commercial purpose in a manner whereby juveniles may examine and peruse"[3] it. The material did not have to reach the bar of "obscene"; it only had to be deemed "harmful" to juveniles.

On July 19, a coalition of booksellers, bookstore owners, publishers, and private citizens filed a complaint in federal court. Bookstore owners argued that the law was so broad in its reach, and vague in specifics, that it would mean having to remove some of the most popular and best-selling authors from their window displays and shelves. Nor could the books be sold in supermarkets, airports, or convenience stores.

They argued that the law was unconstitutional, depriving adults and minors access to literature that, while sexually oriented, was not obscene; a clear infringement of the First Amendment.

While U.S. District Judge Richard L. Williams did not immediately block the law, he said that at the first instance of police trying to enforce the ban he would issue an injunction preventing stopping them if "some member of the Moral Majority should bring a motion for him to enforce the law."[4] He wanted any action to wait while the constitutionality of the law was determined by the Circuit Court.

One bookstore owner named Carol Johnson noted, "I believe it means we will not be able to display or shelve any book or periodical which contains a narrative description or picture of sexual conduct or nudity," which would mean bookstore owners "would have to remove or butcher at least three areas of specialization: parenting and psychology, fiction and mysteries." Johnson also pointed out that some books by Judy Blume and Norma Klein "are not appropriate for 8-year-olds, but they are indeed appropriate for young people, ages 14 and up."[5]

Plaintiff attorney Robert Plotkin added, "If you take it literally, it could reduce material available to people to what is only appropriate to a 10-year-old," said Plotkin. "It's overkill; that's my concern."[6]

But to some, Blume's books were not suitable for children of any age. And her detractors even included government officials: then White House director of communications, Patrick Buchanan, criticized Blume for suggesting that masturbation is normal.

Judith Krug, an executive with the American Library Association, admits that intimations that Blume was immoral irritated her. "She's probably one of the most moral writers for children and young people, which is exactly why she's so popular." Krug says Blume uses their language and her stories deal "with their problems in a totally non-condescending way."[7]

Blume thinks the effort to prevent kids from reading her books is a lot of wasted energy because "they always find a way to read what they are interested in."[8]

It's ironic that Blume was also attacked by some for being too traditional. One critic noted that except for *Deenie*, the perspective of her books was "virtually untouched by the women's movement. . . . Not one [of her girl characters] fights the feminist fight. . . . Sex roles are rarely questioned." The fact that her characters were largely white and suburban also made some question her sensitivity. "Blume's treatment of ethnic and racial issues is equally wanting and limited in scope."[9]

Author Judith Goldberger believes complaints over what isn't in Blume's books detracts from their real value. "Many of today's children have found a source of learning in Judy Blume. . . . She tells them there is a time at which each person must decide things for him or herself. In that sense, she carries an ageless message about the sanctity of individual rights."[10]

Because she touched a chord in her young readers, they frequently sought her out as a sounding board. Sometimes the letters she received were funny, but often they were filled with pleas for help. "I didn't know how to deal with it and I let it paralyze me; the responsibility overwhelmed me," she admits. "I had to get help to find out what I could do. . . . I wanted to save all those needy kids."[11]

Many letters were from kids worried about fights they witnessed between their parents or fretting over a looming divorce. Some thanked her for writing It's Not the End of the World because it helped them get through their own family situations. But even though they adjusted to divorce, they still felt a deep loss. Divorce was always much harder when it was unexpected. Some parents are so good at hiding their problems and never arguing in front of their kids that when they split, it hits the kids like a sucker punch.

Judy says she's not entirely sure why so many kids confide in her on such a personal level. "I know that it's often easier to confide in someone you don't have to face at the breakfast table the next morning, someone who can't use anything you have to say against you," she muses. She also knows from reading the letters that kids believe she understands them on a very basic, fundamental level, "without judging or condemning them for their thoughts and feelings."[12]

In 1986, Judy compiled some of the thousands of letters she had received over the years into a book, Letters to Judy: What Kids Wish They Could Tell You. All the author royalties, or money she made from book sales, was donated to her Kids Fund organization. Her point in publishing the letters was mostly to remind adults that just listening to their children can be the most important thing.

A lot of the letters deal with bullying. Blume notes that if an adult were being harassed in the workplace, the adult could sue (because there are laws against harassment), or simply quit and look for another job. Children do not have that option, she points out. But she believes comfort and understanding at home can help them cope better through rough patches at school.

Although the book, and raising money for Kids Fund, were important to Judy, she found doing the book tour—visiting different cities to sign autographs and do interviews about the book—more difficult than in the past. She admitted that there were other things she'd rather be doings, such as writing. "But I've never been able to do two things at once,"[13] she says, so when on tour, the writing stops.

Compiling *Letters to Judy* was like taking a trip back through time. Reading letters from kids, seeing how important the books were—and how important they remain to new readers just discovering Blume—gave Judy pause. At the time she was writing books like *Margaret* and *Blubber* she was just being instinctual. "I say to myself, *How did I know those things?* I was writing in a natural, spontaneous way then."[14]

It's ironic that the more Judy learned about the craft and mechanics of writing, the less spontaneous it became. "Now it's labor for me," she acknowledges. "Publishers keep saying, *Give us another book, another book.* And that would be lucrative. But I can't work that quickly anymore. I don't want to."[15]

Blume doesn't want to give the impression that she considers herself an authority on children's problems. She freely admits her own children didn't always come to her with their problems during the time she was preoccupied with two bad marriages. It pains her to know that she may have inadvertently not been there for her kids and sent them the message: "I cannot take one more thing, so, please, I don't want to know because I can't handle it."[16]

But the point of *Letters to Judy* isn't to set herself up as the final word. She just wanted to offer insight to both parents and their children. If she has an agenda, it's to encourage more communication between kids and adults. She worries that kids feel like they have to face all their problems alone because they think nobody is listening to them. So they use a letter to Blume as an outlet; a replacement for a parent or sibling at home to unload on.

"I've found them to be respectful and not very demanding," she says. "And not all of them are looking for an answer when they write. There are just some things they want to get out." She says it's not necessarily that the parents aren't listening; because children don't want to disappoint the people who matter most, sometimes they keep their problems bottled up or just "tell their parents what they think the parents want to hear."[17]

Whether one liked or disliked Blume as an author, *Letters to Judy* gave a clear insight into the lives of children. Advice columnist Elizabeth

Winship said the book "might well help [parents and children] into genuine conversation. The book is not a how-to manual, but one compassionate and popular author's way to help parents see life through their children's eyes, and feel it through their hearts and souls."[18]

Writer Faith McNulty came to a similar conclusion after reviewing the book. "I find much in Blume to be thankful for," she said. "She writes clean, swift, unadorned prose. She has convinced millions of young people that truth can be found in a book and that reading is fun. At a time that many believe may be the twilight of the written word, those are things to be grateful for."[19]

It was that, plus her candor and kindheartedness, that made her longtime agent Dick Jackson like Blume the moment she walked into his office back in the late 1960s. Jackson published the books that would later bring her so much scrutiny and criticism. "Judy was a ground-breaker in that 'taboo' subjects just arose naturally from and within her stories,"[20] he said in 2003.

Not everyone who writes to the author is a child. Blume says *Letters to Judy* elicited a response from people in their twenties and thirties who, like the characters in her books, had grown up beset by worries. She says many of them comment, "All that time I thought I was so different and . . . I was really OK. If only I had known then."[21]

Blume says these young adults are looking forward to being better parents because of it. "Like every generation, they say *I'm going to do a better job*," Judy observes. "But they may. They may decide they'll be more open with their kids and accessible."[22]

Inevitably, there are some letters that deal with issues that go way beyond the scope of typical childhood traumas, such as sexual abuse. An emotional woman by nature, Judy got so involved with the kids writing her that she was in danger of cracking under the burden. She admits that she ended up going into therapy to learn how to maintain a necessary personal distance.

Even if Judy couldn't be the personal best friend of every child who wrote her, she could still be their comfort, through her books. And almost twenty years into her career, a new generation of kids was learning about themselves through books like *Margaret*. "It's hard to find a Judy Blume on the shelf anywhere," observed one Seattle library worker. "She is one of the few authors children ask for by name."[23]

And in May 1987, Judy Blume started reaching children via a new medium: theater. The Seattle Children's Theatre presented an adaptation of *Tales of a Fourth Grade Nothing* at the Poncho Theatre. Playwright Bruce Mason, who wrote the adaptation, said prior to the opening, "This is the first time Judy has released one of her books for adaptation to any other medium. I'm told that *Tales of a Fourth Grade Nothing* is the most checked-out book at the Seattle Public Library. I also know that tickets for the weekday school performances of the stage adaptation are going fast, if not already gone." Blume remained a mostly hands-off observer, says Mason, who only spoke with her once. "We talked about everything for 30 or 45 minutes. I had a great time talking to her."[24]

The year 1987 was significant in other ways, both professionally and personally. While Blume continued to reach children through her books, Kids Fund continued to help kids cope with their world. In July 1987, Kids Fund provided a grant to a Chicago area hotline for teenagers that used trained teens to answer the phones. Most importantly, she and George Cooper finally got married on June 6. She also established the Kids Fund at Kean College in Union, New Jersey, furthering the reach of her organization.

Significant to her professionally were the censorship battles being fought in schools. In January 1987, the *Washington Post Magazine* ran the headline: "A Chilling Case of Censorship." The first sentence read: "Last year, teachers in Panama City, Florida, got an award; this year they are getting death threats."[25]

The teachers in question were Gloria Pipkin and ReLeah Lent. And their problems began when they assigned two books by Robert Cormier to their students: *I Am the Cheese* and *The Chocolate War*, the latter being one of the 100 most frequently challenged books because of language and sexuality.

Prior to assigning the book, Pipkin had discussed it with the school principal. With her approval, Pipkin wrote the parents, gave a brief description of the book and invited the parents to read it themselves. Anyone who did not want their child reading the book could have an alternate book assigned to their child. She also informed parents there would be a discussion and invited them to attend. Only one parent showed up and in the end, although she didn't particularly like the book, she allowed her child to participate.

But then came a barrage of criticism. One parent took out a half-page ad in the local paper that included some out of context excerpts. The ad's headline was: "Your Child's Textbooks—Have You Read Them?" It urged parents to petition the school board to remove *The Chocolate War* and all other "obscene" books from the school district. That resulted in a formal complaint against *I Am the Cheese*.

In the end 91 out of 95 parents gave permission for their children to study the book. Despite that and, as Pipkin recounted, "our department's longstanding policy [that] . . . those who found the book objectionable for whatever reason would be given other options," the school superintendent banned the book. "We were devastated," Pipkin says.[26]

Blume understands the frustration. "The way to instill values in children is to talk about difficult issues and bring them out in the open, not to restrict their access to books that may help them deal with their problems and concerns."[27]

The following year a new book selection policy was introduced that forbade material deemed vulgar, obscene, or of a sexual nature. The school superintendent used the policy to remove sixty-five books. Among the banned books were *Hamlet, King Lear, Merchant of Venice, The Red Badge of Courage,* and *The Great Gatsby,* along with the usual suspects including *Of Mice and Men* and *To Kill a Mockingbird.*

It took Pipkin five years and a federal lawsuit to get the banned books reinstated. But during that time, the battle became so heated that Pipkin and a reporter covering the story found themselves physically threatened. The battle, and the isolation Pipkin felt from other teachers, took its toll. She eventually resigned.

This was one of Blume's greatest worries—that censorship of books became censorship of people. Just as it had to Pipkin, "Your favorite teacher, the one who made literature come alive for you, the one who helped you find exactly the book you needed when you were curious, or hurting, the one who was there to listen to you when you felt alone, could become the next target."[28]

It would become Judy's mission to make sure average Americans were aware of what exactly was at stake.

NOTES

1. Judy Blume, *The Pain and the Great One,* (Bradbury, 1984), http://www.judyblume.com/pain.html.

2. New York Public Library (online), *Author Chat with Judy Blume,* November 19, 2002, http://teenlink.nypl.org/blume_txt.html.

3. Caryle Murphy, "Merchandisers Challenge Book Display Ban," *The Washington Post,* July 17, 1985, B8.

4. Caryle Murphy, "Judge Bars Book Law Enforcement," *The Washington Post,* July 20, 1985, C1.

5. Ibid.

6. Ibid.

7. Randy Sue Coburn, "A Best-Selling But Much-Censored Author," *San Francisco Chronicle,* August 12, 1985, p. 15.

8. Ibid.

9. Agnes Garrett and Helga P. McCue, *Authors and Artists for Young Adults*, vol. 3 (Farmington Hills, Mich.: Thomson Gale, 1989), http://www.bookrags.com/biography/judy-blume-aya/.

10. Ibid.

11. Ellen Kanter, "Helping Kids Deal with Divorce," *San Francisco Chronicle*, May 1, 1986, People Section, p. 27.

12. Judy Blume, "Letters Address Children's Secret Feelings," *Chicago Tribune*, May 4, 1986, Tempo, pg. 1.

13. Herbert A. Michelson, "Kids Tell Her Their Secrets," *Sacramento Bee*, May 5, 1986, B03.

14. Ibid.

15. Ibid.

16. Sue Corbett, "Judy Blume Tackles Kids and Money in Her Hero's Latest Adventures," *Miami Herald*, January 15, 2003, http://www.highbeam.com/doc/1G1–119242588.html.

17. Herbert A. Michelson, "Kids Tell Her Their Secrets," *Sacramento Bee*, May 5, 1986.

18. "Biography on Judy Blume," *Encyclopedia of World Biography*, http://www.bookrags.com/biography/judy-blume/.

19. Faith McNulty, "Children's Books for Christmas," *The New Yorker*, December 5, 1983, p. 208.

20. Sue Corbett, "Judy Blume Tackles Kids and Money in Her Hero's Latest Adventures," *Miami Herald*, January 15, 2003, http://www.highbeam.com/doc/1G1–119242588.html.

21. Marsha King, "Writing Wrongs," *Seattle Times*, March 16, 1987, p. C1.

22. Ibid.

23. Ibid.

24. Wayne Johnson, "Blume Book Is Adapted For Seattle Stage," *Seattle Times*, March 13, 1987, Tempo Section, p. 14.

25. ReLeah Lent and Gloria Pipkin, "We Keep Pedaling," *The Alan Review*, 28, no. 2 (Winter 2001), http://scholar.lib.vt.edu/ejournals/ALAN/v28n2/lent.html.

26. Ibid., 9.

27. Agnes Garrett and Helga P. McCue, *Authors and Artists for Young Adults*, vol. 3 (Farmington Hills, Mich.: Thomson Gale, 1989), http://www.bookrags.com/biography/judy-blume-aya/.

28. Jennifer Goldblatt, "Blume's Day," *New York Times*, November 14, 2004, p. 1.

Chapter 9

SPEAKING OUT

Judy says her life changed the day she met Leanne Katz, the first director of the National Coalition Against Censorship. Founded in 1974, NCAC is an alliance, or partnership, between fifty different nonprofit organizations that all have one goal in common: "that freedom of thought, inquiry, and expression must be defended."[1]

Their mandate, or reason to exist, is to defend the First Amendment and to educate the public about the dangers of censorship. The NCAC believes that censorship ultimately threatens not just artistic freedom.

"Freedom of communication is the indispensable condition of a healthy democracy," says the NCAC on its Web site. "In a pluralistic society it would be impossible for all people at all times to agree on the value of all ideas; and fatal to moral, artistic and intellectual growth if they did."[2] Censorship could also be used to quash a person's political or religious views.

> They that can give up essential liberty to obtain a little temporary safety deserve neither liberty nor safety.
>
> —*Benjamin Franklin*

Blume calls Katz, who died in 1997, her hero because she helped normal, everyday people who took a stand against censorship. "Every day she worked with the teachers, librarians, parents and students caught in the cross fire. Many put themselves and their jobs on the line fighting for what they believed in," Judy says.[3]

She recalled the Florida State University professor having to defend classics by Chaucer and Aristophanes against the charge that the books promoted pornography and women's liberation. That same professor also found herself fighting against efforts to ban a student production of *A Raisin in the Sun*.

In St. Louis, a high school English teacher named Cecilia Lacks was fired for allowing students to use street language for a writing assignment. Another English teacher, Alfred Wilder, was fired in Colorado for showing the film *1900* by Bernardo Bertolucci while teaching about fascism. And of special upset to Blume, a Wisconsin guidance counselor was fired for strenuously objecting to the board of education's decision to ban *Forever* from the local junior high. Although the man sued and won, the experience was traumatic.

Judy was involved with several organizations involved with the censorship issue but had a special relationship with NCAC, which was based in New York. "As soon as they hear of any book that's been challenged, they will contact the author and try to work with everyone involved," Blume explains. Even though NCAC was small, she says it was "wonderfully effective." While Blume singled out the ALA and People for the American Way as important organizations in the efforts to limit censorship, she noted that those groups are also "involved in many other activities. The National Coalition deals only with censorship."[4]

She urged anyone who wanted to get involved to "Take a firm stance. Be aware. Don't look the other way. Censors work off fear, and fear is contagious. If you give in to one person's demand, you will find yourself giving into many peoples' demands, and we will be left with nothing." She also encouraged people to support NCAC because it helped "the little guys—the teachers, librarians, students and parents who are under siege." And those people are important because "it only takes one really committed person to make a huge difference."[5]

Fortunately for Blume, her next book, *Just as Long as We're Together*, mostly avoided any censorship controversy (although one library did ban it because a character utters a four-letter curse word). In the story, twelve year-old Stephanie is about to enter seventh grade. Her father is away on an extended business trip. The rest of her family has just moved to a new but smaller house in the same neighborhood where Rachel Robinson lives, Stephanie's best friend since second grade.

Stephanie and Rachel befriend Alison Monceau, who has moved there from Los Angeles. A Vietnamese orphan, Alison was adopted by a well-known actress and her first husband. She's in Connecticut while her mother films a TV series. Living with them are her mom's second husband and Alison's step-grandmother. Alison successfully forges a friendship with both the other girls.

> She knows, of course, but she doesn't want to know. She's very, very angry. She's angry that her parents haven't been honest with her. She's angry at her father for leaving.
>
> —*Just as Long as We're Together*

The first few months of the school year are uneventful. But when Stephanie's dad comes home for Thanksgiving, the truth of his absence turns her world upside down. He has been in California because he and Stephanie's mom are separated and heading for divorce. At Christmas, Stephanie and her brother fly to Los Angeles to visit their father and meet his new girlfriend.

Rather than turn to her friends for comfort, Stephanie keeps her family troubles to herself. The stress causes her to start gaining weight. Her friendship with Rachel begins to suffer, in part from Stephanie's inability to trust her friend with the truth and because of her increasing closeness to Alison. The rift with Rachel is temporary but painful. In the end, Stephanie reconciles with her parents and with her best friend. In the process, she learns that relationships and friendships may not be perfect, but they are resilient. Life always goes on, even if it doesn't go on quite the same way we want it to.

Blume says she had these characters in her mind years before she wrote the book. "So by the time I started I knew them well, or thought I did. I like it best when my characters surprise me as I'm writing, and these three and their families definitely did. Since there are three main characters— Stephanie, Rachel and Alison—I planned to write a trilogy, giving each of the girls her own book. And that still might happen. It's just happening a lot more slowly than I imagined."[6]

When Judy started writing, she and George were spending several days a week at an old house in Westport, Connecticut. That house was the inspiration for the book's setting and some of the story elements. She named some of the characters after Westport stores and businesses. Blume took a picture of a dog belonging to the owner of a local furniture store and an artist's rendering of that picture was used for the original cover.

Blume enjoyed working through problems facing the characters. "I love writing about girls' lives when they're right on the edge," she admits. "One minute they act like little kids, the next they're young women." She feels that by putting Stephanie and the others in difficult situations that are out of their control, "I get to see how they cope and so do my readers."[7]

Judy notes that she uses her characters to address many of the issues she hears in the thousands of letters she receives. "Almost every kid who writes me says something like, *I wish Daddy (or Mommy) could accept me for what I am*. They have this fear that they're not meeting their parents' expectations." She also points out that more and more children are living in stepfamilies than in traditional families. In 1990, when the book was written, one out of every three children no longer lived in an intact nuclear family. "We're making a mess of it. It's the hardest kind of relationship and we need a lot of help."[8]

Some critics were endlessly annoyed that Blume did not neatly wrap up her stories with specific, moral-of-the-story finality. But author Robert Lipsyte says that's precisely why her books remain so relevant.

"Blume explores the feelings of children in a nonjudgmental way. The immediate resolution of a problem is never as important as what the protagonist . . . will learn about herself by confronting her life." Lipsyte believes that young readers gain "from the emotional adventure story both by observing another youngster in a realistic situation and by finding a reference from which to start a discussion with a friend or parent or teacher. For many children, talking about a Blume story is a way to expose their own fears about menstruation or masturbation or death."[9]

R. A. Siegal agrees and says not providing answers doesn't mean the books are not enlightening. "It does not seem that Blume's books ought to be discussed and evaluated on the basis of what they teach children about handling specific social or personal problems . . . they are, after all, works of fiction and not self-help manuals."[10]

Just as Long as We're Together was dedicated to Stephen Murphy. Judy had first met him when he was twelve years old. He was attending Vassar College when she started to write the book. A short time later he was diagnosed with leukemia. She asked him if it was okay to dedicate the book to him. "He laughed about the subject matter—three girls in seventh grade—but gave me his blessing."[11] Stephen died before the book was published.

In 1988 Judy and her son Larry collaborated on what she calls a labor of love. They produced a low-budget film version of *Otherwise Known as Sheila the Great*. The movie was financed by an educational film company. Judy cowrote and coexecutive-produced the movie with Larry, who also directed it. "It's fun when the characters speak your lines and it works. . . . We had wonderful kids. It's charming and it works."[12] The film was later bought by ABC and broadcast as a Weekend Special.

Judy says it's her favorite adaptation of any of her books. "I love the result. And I just think we were able to catch something, even on no budget to speak of. The whole thing was done in a few days. I felt it spoke in a special way. It wasn't sitcom. It wasn't all jokes." Although she enjoyed the experience, she admits it was very time consuming. So the only way she could be that involved again was "if I didn't want to write any more books."[13]

In February 1989, Blume's daughter Randy, then a pilot for Continental Airlines, married David Pickle, an Air Force meteorologist. The ceremony was presided over by Justice Helen Freedman of the New York State Supreme Court and took place at the James Burden Mansion in Manhattan. The historic house is located on the Upper East Side near Central Park. It was designed by the same architects responsible for Grand Central Station.

Later that year, Randy quit Continental because she wanted to start a family. She recalls her obstetrician commenting that it would be difficult getting pregnant when she was never home. Plus, she admits her long hours were a strain on her marriage. "And the airline lifestyle was not the way I wanted to raise a child," Randy says.[14]

Writing must run in the blood. After leaving the airline, Randy was commissioned to write a book about her life as a pilot. But instead of an autobiography, the publisher asked her to write a novel. So just like her mother, Randy used her own real-life experiences to create a book. But unlike her mother, Randy's book, *Crazy in The Cockpit: A Woman Pilot's Adventures in the Air,* was ignored by censors. However, compared to what was happening to some writers, Judy's experiences were mild.

Author Salman Rushdie had to go into hiding after a religious leader in Iran issued a *fatwa,* or religious edict, calling for Rushdie's assassination because of his novel, *The Satanic Verses,* which many Muslims considered irreverent. Still, when a group of authors congregated at the Atlanta-Fulton Public Library to show support for Rushdie by reading excerpts from *The Satanic Verses* out loud, they also read passages from several Judy Blume books.

At the time, then-NCAC President Leanne Katz noted, "The attacks on Judy come in large part because she's writing about things kids care about," says Katz—including girls who take responsibility for their own sexuality "outside of the context of their being victims," Katz emphasizes.

GETTING ORGANIZED

In an age when militants are showing new strength in their efforts to crush contrary ideas, American booksellers find themselves not just merchants but moral mediators as well.

Book banning and other forms of intellectual harassment, like those efforts now aimed at art, are current and proliferating. And booksellers are getting organized to cope with their new role as First Amendment police.[15]

—Charles Trueheart, *The Washington Post*

At the annual American Booksellers Association convention in 1990, the formation of the ABA Foundation for Free Expression was announced. The group's mandate is to educate the public about First Amendment issues and to respond officially to local censorship incidents. While most of the censorship efforts came from the religious right, according to a report by Charles Trueheart in *The Washington Post,* there had been an increase in similar efforts from what he termed the "feminist and ethnic left."[16]

He cited a case in Bellingham, Washington where a feminist activist was lobbying to have an issue of *Esquire* removed from a local bookstore because of the cover story, "The Secret Life of the American Wife," which included a section titled, "Your Wife: An Owner's Manual."

The bookstore's owner, Chuck Robinson, acknowledged that the article may offend some women's modern-day sensibilities but added, "They are nonetheless ideas . . ."[17]

Sometimes it seems as if the goal of censors is to so completely homogenize ideas that creative thought is eradicated. In 2002, a "sensitivity committee" altered passages from literature that were part of New York State's Regents exams, which are standardized tests all high school students must take before they can graduate. Judy and other members of the National Coalition Against Censorship called a press conference to protest. "It's amazing that some of the finest literature for high school students was chosen, and then it was put through a committee that decided to remove everything that made it what it is," Blume stated. "All references to race, religion, body size were taken out. It's bizarre."[18]

The author said sometimes it seemed the censors were attacking from all sides. "You have the evangelical right wanting these books removed, and the (politically correct) crowd wanting these books removed, and the sensitivity team wanting everything removed. What will we be left with? It's disgusting."[19]

NOTES

1. National Coalition Against Censorship, http://www.ncac.org/about/about.cfm (accessed July 13, 2007).

2. Ibid.

3. Judy Blume, ed., *Places I Never Meant To Be* (New York: Simon & Shuster, 1999), http://www.judyblume.com/articles/places-intro.html.

4. Ibid.

5. Random House Interview, http://www.randomhouse.com/boldtype/0698/blume/interview.html (accessed July 13, 2007).

6. Judy Blume, *Just as Long as We're Together,* (London: Orchard Books, 1987), http://www.judyblume.com/just-as.html.

7. Ibid.

8. Carol Felsenthal, "Judy Blume Grows Up," American Library Assn. March 27, 1984, http://www.newspaperarchive.com/PdfViewer.aspx?img=14689639&firstvisit=true&src=search&currentResult=5&currentPage=0.

9. Robert Lipsyke, "A Bridge of Words," *The Nation,* November 21, 1981, http://content.epnet.com/pdf17_20/pdf/1981/NAT/21Nov81/11241769.pdf?T=P&P=AN&K=11241769&EbscoContent=dGJyMMvl7ESeprA4yOvqOLCmrk%2bepq9Sr6m4TLWWxWXSAAAA&ContentCustomer=dGJyMPLe44bf6ueH7KTreefkrH3m5fGMAAAA&S=R&D=nih.

10. *Lion and the Unicorn* 2, no. 2 (Fall 1978).

11. Judy Blume, *Just as Long as We're Together,* (London: Orchard Books, 1987), http://www.judyblume.com/just-as.html.

12. Sue Corbett, "Judy Blume Tackles Kids and Money in Her Hero's Latest Adventures," *Miami Herald,* January 15, 2003, http://www.highbeam.com/doc/1G1–119242588.html.

13. Ibid.

14. Michael Kenney, "Air Apparent Randy Blume Talks About Her Love of Flying, Her First Novel, and Her Mother, Judy, Who Prefers Land," *Boston Globe,* May 25, 1999, E1.

15. Charles Trueheart, "Booksellers & The Battle Joined; Anti-Censorship Foundation Formed," *Washington Post,* June 5, 1990, C1.

16. Ibid.

17. Ibid.

18. Mary Grossman, "Blume Doesn't Sound Too Convincing When She Talks About Retiring," *Knight Ridder/Tribune News Service,* October 9, 2002, http://www.highbeam.com/doc/1G1–92666343.html.

19. Joseph P. Kahn, "The Heat At The Vineyard," *Boston Globe,* July 6, 1995.

Chapter 10

REDUX

Fudge was the character that wouldn't go away. Judy Blume assumed she had written the last of the Hatchers with *Superfudge* in 1980. Even though scores of fans wrote asking her, some begging her, to write another book about the younger brother from hell, she didn't have any ideas . . . until she and George spent the summer of 1989 in Southwest Harbor, Maine. "As soon as we pulled up to the old shingled house and I saw the rope swing hanging from the tree, I imagined Sheila Tubman swinging on it and the idea came to me—Peter's family and Sheila's family would spend their summer vacation sharing a house in Maine."[1]

Judy admits that having worked on the *Otherwise Known as Sheila the Great* movie had made her want to write about Sheila again. The Maine setting made it the perfect background. "I don't think I could set a book in a place without knowing it really well,"[2] Blume says.

Again told from Peter's perspective, this is not his idea of a dream vacation. As if living next door to Sheila isn't bad enough, Fudge has announced his plans to marry Peter's nemesis when he grows up. It was a set-up that gave Judy ample opportunity for humor.

Blume's agent, Stephanie Laurie, says her client "is the strongest comedy writer I've ever worked with." She credits Blume with having the skill to set up a situation then deliver the perfectly worded punch line. "She has a perfect ear for dialogue. She has her finger on the pulse of middle-grade readers. She knows what embarrasses them, and how they feel about the opposite sex and about parents. That's what makes her books timeless."[3]

Earlier in her career Blume admits she used to be superstitious talking about where she got her ideas. She was afraid if she ever figured it out, she'd never have another one. "But now I know that ideas come from everywhere—memories of my own life, incidents in my children's lives, what I see and hear and read—and most of all, from my imagination."[4]

Judy says writing comedy isn't as easy as it may seem. For her, books often arise from a situation. "If you're writing about a character in a situation, the story will naturally grow," she explains. By comparison, "Writing a funny book is much more difficult." But, she acknowledges, "I never lost my ability to laugh at a kid's joke, to just go with it."[5]

Sometimes, the results surprise Blume. "When I first wrote about Fudge and his family in *Tales of a Fourth Grade Nothing*, the characters and the stories were more cartoon like than realistic," she says. Then by the time she wrote *Fudge-a-Mania*, "it was still about the humor, but both the story lines and the characters were growing more and more real."[6]

Even though Peter and Fudge appear in several books, Judy does not consider the books part of a Fudge series, the way *Harry Potter* or the *Series of Unfortunate Events* are. She claims she wouldn't be good writing a series and says the only reason it happened with Fudge was mostly because of reader demand. "And I'm not sure that's the best way to write a book," she muses. After *Fudge-a-Mania* she thought, "I'll bring them all together and then I'll be done with it. I'll never have to do it again."[7]

The summer Judy and George spent in Maine was cold and rainy. Blume says that personally it was disappointing that the weather wasn't better, but professionally, it was very conducive to writing her next Fudge book. Setting the book in Southwest Harbor, Judy used the names of real local shops and even some local people in the book. "There really was a guy everyone called Bicycle Bob," she says. "I bought a bike from him that summer. We grocery shopped at Sawyer's Market on Main Street, and spent time browsing at Oz Books, a children's book store."[8]

Judy's husband suggested the title, but as *Fudge-a-Maine-ia*. But in the end, it ended up being spelled the usual way. After she finished the book, Judy says she told everyone not to expect another Fudge book. Ever. Of course Judy would learn never to say never . . .

MARTHA'S VINEYARD

In 1992, Judy and George bought a house in Martha's Vineyard. They also have a home in Key West, Florida, and a New York City apartment that overlooks the Hudson River. "Only islands, George likes to say,"[9] jokes Judy.

Living in New York City is a bit of a dream come true for the New Jersey native. As a young child, Blume attended a summer camp with several girls who lived in Manhattan on the city's Upper West Side. During the year, the girls would get together for a mini-reunion and Judy would spend the night in the city. She and her friend would walk along Broadway. "It was so exciting, seeing all the people and street life,"[10] she recalls.

When in New York, Judy still walks up and down Broadway. She also takes tap dance classes, which are a special passion for her. "The class is made up of young hopefuls and me, and I'm putting myself on the line. While I'm there, I don't think about another thing."[11]

They now spend four months—May through September—of every year at their two-acre Martha's Vineyard estate, which has one main house and four guest cottages that are usually filled with family and friends. The house is nestled beside Lake Tashmoo and perched at the end of a long, unpaved road, ensuring Judy's privacy.

Her time on Martha's Vineyard was one of studied relaxation, where her usual attire consists of shorts, T-shirt, and sandals. On a typical day, she writes during the mornings in a small cabin located a short distance from the main house. She writes one scene at a time, referring back to the notebook she keeps for every story. She calls the notebook her security blanket because it keeps her from facing a blank page alone.

After that she spends time riding her bike, kayaking, or taking a walk. She also spends time daydreaming. Blume says being on the Vineyard "remind[s] me of those long, lazy summer days when you just lay on your back and looked at the clouds, making things up. Being by yourself. I still think that's the most important thing a writer can have."[12]

She notes that her ideas never come when sitting at her desk. If she has a regret, it's that "I seem to have less and less time for just sitting and reading! I really miss that time to myself to get lost in a good book."[13]

Blume recalls the authors and books that influenced her writing: Beverly Cleary, Louise Fitzhugh's *Harriet the Spy*, and E. L. Konigsberg. What they all have in common is strong characters. "I like to know what's inside their heads. And when I'm writing, the same thing is true. For me, character is everything. I'm interested in people and how they cope and how they relate."[14] She's also interested in families because dealing with families is something that everyone can relate to.

As much as writing informs who she is, Judy admits that it's not always fun because, "It's a solitary life and it can get lonely. You spend most of the day in a little room by yourself. But since I love to create characters and get to know them, I'm usually content." Blume's characters are so realistic that some people assume she is writing about real people, but the author assures, "while they feel real to me, I've actually made them up."[15]

Despite her love of Martha's Vineyard, Blume considers Key West, Florida, her primary home and can't imagine ever leaving it. "We're so in love with this community,"[16] she says. "We have more parties here than I have ever been to in my life. It's like junior high school but without all the bad stuff,"[17] she jokes, adding that the community attracts a lot of writers.

The balmy Key West weather appeals to Judy. "I love summer. That's why I'm here." Just as in Martha's Vineyard, Judy tools around Key West on her bicycle. "I'm a kid and I get to play and nobody tells me what to do and when to go home."[18]

Judy admits that her full life has put a crimp in her writing. She wishes she could write as fast as she reads because normally it takes her a year to write a book. The hardest part is the first draft, which she calls "torture." But once she has a full manuscript, she sees it as having "the pieces to the puzzle. I love to put it together and make it into a whole."[19]

One thing Judy says she doesn't believe in is writer's block. She says there can be good days and bad days writing and on those bad days, she'll get out of the office and go for a walk or just sit by the water and think. And if she still can't come up with the words or the dialogue, she knows it'll be better the next day.

But even as she writes the first draft, Judy says she edits the book as she goes. One of her tricks is to put the manuscript aside for a couple of weeks, then take it out and read it out loud. She also works very closely with her editor. She believes good editors can point out sections or scenes that don't work because they are looking at them objectively.

The one thing writing a book requires is time. When she complained to a friend that it was hard finding time to write, the friend told her, "You've got too many floor plans in your life," which she admits very well may be true. Blume calls herself a "nest-builder" and says she like to move around. "Every few years the bug bites. Yes, it's a great excuse not to write. And yes, it can be a creative high. But at the end of the day there's no new book."[20]

Somewhat surprisingly, Blume has thought about retiring from writing and taking a regular nine-to-five job . . . mostly because she's never had one. She's never had to set the alarm clock to get up and go work for someone else. The reason the fantasy appeals to her is because "It's difficult not to have structure in your life." On the other hand, she quickly acknowledges, it would be very difficult "to give up the freedom I have."[21]

Since he retired from being a teacher, Blume's husband George had also turned to writing. His specialty was writing books about historical (nonfiction) crimes and trials. Judy says George calls her lucky because she gets to "make things up. I think it would be fun to do research and discover stories, like George."[22]

But in a way Blume does do research: by listening and observing. Once her own children were grown, Judy worried that her days of writing for children might be over and she admits sometimes she feels a little removed from adolescents on occasion—until she spends time with a group of youths. Then, she says, "I feel like it's exactly the same. So I think it has something to do with the way you see the world, you know? We're all a certain age inside. And I guess those of us to hang on to the really early ages are the ones who feel most comfortable writing about it."[23]

When asked if she ever worried that her books sound dated because slang among today's adolescents is different from what it was thirty years ago, Judy disagreed with the premise of the question. She doesn't believe "trendy" language is what makes the makes the books believable and relatable; it's that they speak to the reader on an emotional level. "My earliest readers are in their 30s now," Blume comments, "and I'm still getting the same number of letters from today's 10-year-olds. So I guess that trendy isn't what it's all about."[24]

Another thing that hadn't changed was the ongoing debate over censoring books children might read. What had begun as an issue primarily confined to school libraries had expanded to public libraries—something that surprised Blume when she learned of it. Prior to the National Coalition Against Censorship, it was hard to ascertain information about banning efforts unless she or other authors happened to read about it in the paper. "I don't think any school board or school library or teacher has ever tried to contact me directly."[25]

In 1991, Blume traveled to Seattle to speak at the National Council of Teachers annual meeting. She was dismayed to discover how unprepared teachers and school librarians were in knowing how to respond to censorship. Few had any policy or strategies in place, meaning they would not have an efficient, organized response. Judy gave the attendees the names and phone number of support groups. "I'm not aware of what may be going on in public libraries, but the school librarians, teachers, and principals who are under fire should know that they are not alone, that there is a support group." Blume notes that censors will claim that removing a book from a school is ultimately harmless "because a reader can always go to a public library to find it. That's one way the censor is able to get a book out of a school."[26]

Judy equates having a book banned with suffering a loss. "It's like a grieving process," she explains, saying that she goes through different stages, beginning with anger. "What is wrong with these people? How can they possibly think this is something to be afraid of?" But after having had so many experiences, her reaction has changed. "I'm too familiar with it. I'm glad I'm beyond that."[27]

She is also beyond trying to directly defend herself. She recalls the time she agreed to debate a representative from the Moral Majority. Afterward she promised never to put herself in that position again. But she is heartened when she hears of average citizens joining the fight against book banning because it means they care about books and about individual rights and freedoms.

"The point I would like to make is that it is the kids who are the losers in all these battles. We're really talking about what they have a right to know, what they have a right to read." Blume stresses that children have rights, too, and says they "are beginning to understand that they have a right to choose what they want to read. I think it's very positive that they become involved in these struggles within their community. I encourage young people to become involved."[28]

The Reverend Debra Haffner, who served as the chief executive officer of SIECUS—the Sex, Information, and Educational Council of the United States—from 1988 to 2000, agrees with Blume that censorship of books like *Forever* and *Are You There God? It's Me, Margaret* hurt young people. She believed the "bottom line of these programs is to scare kids into abstinence . . . and to withhold information" about an assortment of issues, such as contraception, masturbation, and sexual feelings, and including homosexuality.[29]

At the National Coalition Against Censorship's anticensorship symposium, "The Sex Panic: Women, Censorship and Pornography," Blume gave a speech titled *Is Puberty a Dirty Word?* She read a letter from a thirteen-year-old girl who said, "My mom never talks about the things young girls think most about. She doesn't know how I feel. I don't know where I stand in the world. I don't know who I am. That's why I read—to find myself."[30]

Blume told the attendees, "We have the language police, we have the sex police. We have the adults so worried about everything they have no time to worry about the kids." She read another letter from an incest victim, who told her, "I felt like I didn't deserve anything good to happen to me, ever. I didn't eat much. I would only talk if I had to. I wished myself dead. . . . I bite myself, scratch myself, make myself sick, wishing someone, primarily teachers, would ask me if something was wrong . . . but no one came to me." Nor could the girl bring herself to seek help. "By not having courage, I lost my chance."[31]

Judy said when it came to standing up to censorship, "By not having courage, we all lose our chances."[32]

NOTES

1. Judy Blume, *Fudge-a-Mania*, (New York: Dutton, 1990), http://www.judy blume.com/fudge-a-mania.html.

2. "Authors: Judy Blume," Random House, http://www.randomhouse.com/ author/results.pperl?authorid=2611&view=full_sptlght (accessed July 13, 2007).

3. Ibid.

4. Judy Blume, "Welcome," Judy Blume Official Website, http://www.judy blume.com/message.html.

5. Rosemary Herbert, "A Kid at Heart; Children's Author Judy Blume Brings Back Antics of Fudge," *The Boston Herald*, October 18, 2002, http://www.high beam.com/doc/1G1–93016790.html.

6. Amanda Rogers, "Nine Reasons To Scoop Up Judy Blume's Tales Of Fudge Hatcher," *Fort Worth Star-Telegram*, February 11, 2003, http://www.high beam.com/doc/1G1–119478485.html.

7. "Talk of the Nation: Teens Across America," NPR.org, October 21, 1998, http://www.npr.org/templates/story/story.php?storyId = 1009881.

8. Judy Blume, *Fudge-a-Mania*, (New York: Dutton, 1990), http://www.judy blume.com/fudge-a-mania.html.

9. Joseph P. Kahn, "Judy Blume's Summer Camp," *Boston Globe*, July 6, 1995, Living Section, p. 61.

10. Enid Nemy, "It's Judy Blume, New Yorker," *New York Times*, October 3, 1982, http://select.nytimes.com/search/restricted/article?res=F30711FB345C0C 708CDDA90994DA484D81.

11. Ibid.

12. Ibid.

13. "This Cultural Life," *The Independent*, Sunday, May 29, 2005, http://www. highbeam.com/doc/1P2-1931556.html.

14. Ibid.

15. "Message from Judy Blume," official Judy Blume Web site, http://www. judyblume.com/message.html (accessed July 13, 2007).

16. Sue Corbett, "Judy Blume Tackles Kids and Money in Her Hero's Latest Adventures," *Miami Herald*, January 15, 2003, http://www.highbeam.com/ doc/1G1–119242588.html.

17. "This Cultural Life," *The Independent*, Sunday, May 29, 2005, http://www. highbeam.com/doc/1P2-1931556.html.

18. Ellen Kanner, "Judy Blume," http://www.bookpage.com/9805bp/judy_ blume.html (accessed July 13, 2007).

19. Judy Blume, "Message from Judy," February, 2004, www.judyblume.com.

20. "Authors: Judy Blume," Random House, http://www.randomhouse.com/ author/results.pperl?authorid=2611&view=full_sptlght (accessed July 13, 2007).

21. Enid Nemy, "It's Judy Blume, New Yorker," *New York Times*, October 3, 1982, http://select.nytimes.com/search/restricted/article?res=F30711FB345C0C 708CDDA90994DA484D81.

22. "Talk of the Nation: Teens Across America," NPR.org, October 21, 1998, http://www.npr.org/templates/story/story.php?storyId=1009881.

23. Ibid.

24. Ibid.

25. Herbert N. Foerstel, *Banned in the U.S.A.: A Reference Guide to Book Censorship in Schools and Public Libraries* (Westport: Greenwood Press, 2002), p. 135.

26. Ibid., p 136.

27. Ibid.

28. Ibid.

29. "The Sex Panic, A Conference Report," National Coalition Against Censorship, 1993, http://www.ncac.org/projects/sex_panic.cfm.

30. Ibid.

31. Ibid.

32. Ibid.

Chapter 11

TOGETHER, AGAIN

Judy Blume always begins one of her books on the day some significant event out of the ordinary happens. For example, in *Superfudge*, it was the day Peter learns his mother is pregnant. *Here's to You, Rachel Robinson* starts the day Rachel's troublemaking, older brother Charles gets expelled from boarding school. Rachel, a diligent, straight-A student, must now deal with her brother living back at home and acting out to get his parents' attention.

> Trouble in our family is spelled with a capital C and has been as long as I can remember. The C stands for Charles. He's my older brother, two years and four months older to be exact. Ever since the phone call about him last night, I've felt incredibly tense. . . . I tried to take a deep breath. I read an article about relieving tensions in *Psychology Today*. You take a deep breath, then count to ten as you slowly release it. But as I inhaled, I caught the scent of the fresh lilacs on Ms. Leffert's desk and I started to cough.
>
> —*Here's to You Rachel Robinson*

Rachel and her family were first introduced as one of the three friends in *Just as Long As We're Together*. Blume says she always intended that book to be the first of a trilogy, each featuring one of the friends, and she was especially intrigued with Rachel and her family. But instead of sitting down to write a book about them right away, Judy went on to other projects.

"I think it's that when I finish one kind of book I want my next project to be something totally different."[1]

After compiling the letters for *Letters to Judy* and writing *Fudge-a-Mania*, Blume spent several months developing a television series based on the three girls in *Just As Long As We're Together*. But after all that work, the series never materialized. So by the time Judy turned her attention back to Rachel, several years had passed. She reveals that Rachel's character "was inspired by a friend of mine when I was in junior high, a high achieving perfectionist."[2] She was also inspired by a letter she once received from a twelve-year-old girl who was taking college courses.

Although Judy received the letter several years earlier, it had stuck with her. "It was an interesting idea—that a kid other kids might envy could feel so set apart and lonely because she was brighter than her peers."[3] But in this girl's case, because she was so intellectually advanced, her classmates "didn't want to be her friends anymore. She confided that she'd give it all up just to be a normal girl. I found that letter so sad. But I knew what she was saying. It's hard to feel you're different from your peers."[4]

In addition to her troubled brother, Rachel also has to deal with her older sister Jessica and cope with a work-obsessed parent. Judy acknowledges that of the three friends in *Just As Long As We're Together*, Rachel is probably the character that is least relatable to the vast majority of kids who'll read the book. But she found the complicated family dynamics full of drama and loved writing about it. Although she dedicated the book to her stepdaughter Amanda—who she credits with bringing her and George together—Blume says not to read anything into it. She simply dedicated it to her "for no reason other than to say she's important to me."[5]

While *Here's to You, Rachel Robinson* didn't face the criticism some of Blume's other books did, it wasn't without some controversy. In one scene Charles, an angry fifteen year-old lashing out at those closest to him, swears:

> Here's to you, Rachel Robinson. Here's to my whole f***ing family.
>
> —*Here's to You, Rachel Robinson*

Blume remembers having a lengthy discussion with her agent, who told her that one word "will keep [the book] from being accepted here, here and here."[6] Keeping it in the book meant more than just losing book club sales. "It would be mentioned in every review, making librarians and teachers afraid to order it for their classrooms and school libraries," Blume explained." She began to think maybe it wouldn't be such a bad idea to use another word. "If I changed the word to *frigging*, we might not have a problem. If I changed it to *freaking* we might not have a problem."[7]

Her editor left the final decision to Judy, who agonized over it. She spent several nights laying awake, trying to decide what to do. In her heart, Judy knew the expletive was true to the character; was an honest response. "I knew him very well. He was smart and articulate. He chose his words carefully. He didn't punctuate every sentence with *meaningless word intensifiers*," she says, referring to how her dictionary defined that particular curse word. Even though he causes trouble, Blume cause Charles a "great character," but adds, "I wouldn't want to live with him."[8]

In the end, it was her son Larry who convinced Judy to follow her heart. "My son said: *You're Judy Blume! You're known for being honest. If you don't use the word you want . . . every kid will know you're being dishonest.*" Blume admitted his encouragement made her cry. "Sometimes it's really important to hear that."[9]

In the end, Judy kept the word. And, as expected, she felt some backlash. Several adults, and some children, wrote her to complain. A teacher in Tennessee accused Blume of betrayal for the decision. And in fact, *Rachel Robinson* became the first book designated to be held on a new system of restricted-access library books in the Tennessee county school system.

When Blume responded to the teacher and others, she tried to explain why it wasn't as simple as just replacing a "damn" with a "darn." It's about keeping true to oneself as a writer and true to the characters and story. Moreover, she stresses that there is such thing as a guaranteed safe book.

The seemingly innocuous *Superfudge* was targeted for banning because of a chapter titled *Santa Who?* In it, Fudge, who is five, tells his older brother that he doesn't really believe in Santa Claus, but he pretends to because it pleases their parents. When a music theater company called Theatreworks staged a stage adaptation of *Superfudge*, a group of schools in the south refused to allow the production to perform for their students unless changes were made to that particular scene. Although Judy had the authority to stop Theatreworks from making the changes, she didn't.

"There are times when I'm just too weary to fight. You have to choose your battles." Plus, she pointed out there were several differences between the book and the adaptation—which children were quick to point out to her. In the end, she hoped children who saw the production would be inspired to read the book to meet the Fudge Judy created. Although there were no hard feelings, Blume asks rhetorically, "Would I let them adapt another of my books? Probably not. I was disappointed in them though I understood their dilemma. Non-profits have their own problems."[10]

Of special concern to Judy is that the mere threat of censorship causes people to run scared. "Somebody thinks there will be a controversy, so they avoid the issue by quietly keeping the book out of their town. But let's face it—puberty is not going to go away. Kids need to talk about it."

Blume knows that parents are genuinely concerned, so she tries to put a positive spin on their fears. She asks them, "What's the worst thing that can happen? Your kids will ask questions. You'll talk. If you really feel the material is inappropriate, then by all means, don't have it in the house. But tell your kids why. Talk about these issues in your own way, but talk."[11]

Judy adds, "Though it's hard for kids to believe, growing up is a very universal process. It connects us all. The details change, but the feelings don't." While Judy believes that the feelings and issues she addresses are universal in nature, she says she is a very personal writer. "It's nice to share feelings and experiences, and to touch other people's lives, but I don't write for anyone but myself.[12]

"What I do is certainly not a formula," she says. "It's just my voice. I write about these people and these things because they interest me—or at least the child in me."[13]

By the mid-1990s, however, Blume's literary output was slowing down. Not because she no longer had anything to say, but because the impetus to write had changed. "I used to be real prolific until George came along and ruined my career by making me happy,"[14] she jokes. "All right, it hasn't ruined it, but I don't have the same need. I don't have the same angst. And I think that good writing comes from that kind of angst."[15]

NOTES

1. Judy Blume, *Here's to You Rachel Robinson*, (London: Orchard Books, 1993), http://www.judyblume.com/rachel.html.

2. Ibid.

3. Brooks Whitney, "Judy Blume Gets Real," *Chicago Tribune*, November 23, 1993.

4. Ibid.

5. Ibid.

6. Ibid.

7. RoseEtta Stone, *X-Rated Children's Books*, 1, no. 18 (October 18, 2002).

8. Paula Span, "Late Blumers; A Childhood Favorite's Latest Book, Making Grown Women Read," August 24, 1998, B1.

9. RoseEtta Stone, *X-Rated Children's Books*, 1, no. 18 (October 18, 2002).

10. Ibid.

11. Mary Gillespie, "Words of Wisdom," *Chicago Sun-Times*, October 6, 1993, http://www.highbeam.com/doc/1P2–4193375.html.

12. Enid Nemy, "It's Judy Blume, New Yorker," *New York Times*, October 3, 1982, http://select.nytimes.com/search/restricted/article?res=F30711FB345C0C 708CDDA90994DA484D81.

13. Mary Gillespie, "Words of Wisdom," *Chicago Sun-Times*, October 6, 1993, http://www.highbeam.com/doc/1P2-4193375.html.

14. Joseph P. Kahn, "Judy Blume's Summer Camp," *Boston Globe*, July 6, 1995, Living Section, p. 61.

15. Rebecca Ascher Walsh, "The 'Fudge' Report," *Entertainment Weekly*, October 11, 2002, p. 77.

Chapter 12

FUDGE

Television networks are always on the lookout for material that they can adapt for the small screen. And they are especially eager to attract younger viewers, especially as competing technologies such as the Internet and video games have started taking viewers away from traditional TV. So it's not surprising that Judy frequently got offers from producers wanting to base a program on her books and characters. But Blume was extremely protective of her material. At the same time, she liked the idea of reaching vast numbers of children through a new medium. So when ABC approached her about developing a show around Fudge and the Hatcher family, she agreed. While Judy didn't have qualms about kids watching television, she just wished that the programs offered were better and urged kids not to become couch potatoes.

Rather than an animated series, the network decided to produce a live-action two-hour TV movie, *Fudge-a-Mania*, to launch a weekly Saturday morning series. Judy went into the project with hopeful optimism that all the elements would come together to make the series she envisioned. Although she had been pleased with *Forever*, and thought it was faithful to the emotion of the book, in retrospect she thought it might have been better. "I would have cast a different Michael though," she admits. "I had trouble believing the lovely Stephanie Zimbalist would fall for him."[1]

Judy was even more enthused when the network indicated they wanted her to be closely involved with the project. "They said they needed my input desperately," she recalled. So she and George packed up and relocated to Los Angeles for several months. To her surprise and great frustration, the producers kept her at arm's length.

"They wouldn't let me anywhere near it. It was terrible." She felt completely shoved aside and misled. "It was a great lesson in surviving a degrading, humiliating experience."[2] Judy promised George she wouldn't cry . . . but she did—although, she points out, not every day.

The TV movie aired in December 1994 and the series debuted in 1995. Ironically, despite the bitterly disappointing work experience, Judy found the series acceptable; perhaps because she had left Los Angeles with severely lowered expectations.

"When we went into it we said what we're going for here is the DNE award: Does Not Embarrass," she explains. "And it does not embarrass."[3]

Blume loved the actors that were cast, particularly the children. She also thought the set they built was done extremely well. "I couldn't believe what they were able to build on a lot," she recalls. "The brilliant creative stuff was fun, in that way."[4] What she liked a lot less was how fast they work in television so that everyone was always in such a hurry, some attention to detail was lost.

Overall, Judy was disappointed because she thought it could have been different and better. "I wanted it to be original and wonderful and capture whatever it is about the books that grabbed kids all these years."[5] But she wasn't disappointed enough that she wrote Hollywood off completely. She remained open to the idea of turning another of her books into a movie or series, although Blume says she learned she couldn't let herself get quite so emotionally involved and invested next time.

RECOGNITION

In 1996, Judy Blume was honored with the Margaret A. Edwards Award for Outstanding Literature for Young Adults from the American Library Association. "It is given to an author for lifetime achievement in writing for teenagers, whose work helps teenagers to better understand themselves and their world."[6]

The awards are cosponsored by the *School Library Journal* and the ALA's division, Young Adult Library Services Association (YALSA). The winner, chosen by a five-person committee, is announced at the ALA midwinter conference. The award itself is presented at the ALA annual conference. The award was established in 1988 to honor an author whose works addressed the concerns of adolescents, ages twelve to eighteen. The award is for a specific book, which must have been in print at least five years to be nominated. Blume won for *Forever*.

Margaret Edwards, for whom the award is named, worked at the Enoch Pratt Free Library in Baltimore. She was known for promoting young adult literature to both the public and to skeptical publishers. When asked how she manages to tap so easily into the psyches of young adults, Blume has no ready answer. "I can't really explain how it works," she admits. "You're sitting there and writing and then you read it and say, *How did I do that?*" She says when the words are flowing easily, "You are in some other place."[7]

She also reveals that writing can be extremely cathartic because she can work out her own issues through her characters. "My brother says that I save five years on the psychiatrist's couch with every book I write."[8]

Although Judy knows she has to maintain a certain emotional distance from her fans, she's aware how many kids want her to help them. "The worst letters are the ones threatening suicide and, well, twice now I've answered letters from kids who were sick—physically sick—and the letters arrived after the children had died. God!"[9]

She also shies away from giving general advice to kids and young adults. Judy does think it's important they know that, "Life is full of making mistakes. Mistakes are OK, but it's important to learn from them. Always be responsible for your own actions."[10]

While honored to win the Margaret A. Edwards Award, Blume jokes that it also kind of worried her. "Is this good that they're accepting me? I mean, the whole library thing."[11] Meaning, the whole censorship thing. In a report compiled by People for the American Way that tracked school censorship from 1982 to 1996, Judy Blume topped the Most Challenged Authors list. "Such an odd thing," Judy says, "when you really think about it, that puberty would be taboo for young people to read about."[12]

The award brought out a show of appreciation and support for Blume. Publisher David Fickling considers her books a "wonderful corrective to the rather over-literary children's books" that were common when Judy started writing. "Everyone got offended and no one had read anything nearly as shocking. It was deeply needed. She spoke directly to kids in an emotional way, and of course it was deeply attractive."[13]

Despite the growing sophistication of children, *Forever*, the book cited for the award, remained relevant, which still amazed Judy. "I can't believe I'm still talking about this book twenty years later," she said at the time. "I've said before I don't want any awards because that would mean that they approve of me and therefore the kids won't like me."[14]

But she credits the fact that the basic characters and situations she wrote about reflected the real life of kids. "It's always families, friendships and schools,"[15] she says. And while children don't have the worldly experience or the perspective of an adult, their emotions and feelings are just as intense. That's why it astounds Judy when she gets criticized for writing about personal issues.

"I don't know why adults think children are not interested in those things," she comments, using Randy's son Elliot, who was born in 1992, as an example. Randy and Elliott's dad are divorced and Blume says, "I know that is what is on his mind at the age of five . . . He may pick up the phone and tell me what Lego set he wants for his birthday but I have also heard him say *My mum and dad are separate* and it just broke my heart."[16]

Blume also has a thick skin when critics attack her books for not being *literature*. "I don't care what they say as long as the kids are reading it, and as long as they're identifying, or in some way emotionally involved," she states. "If they're touched by something, care about something, who cares what those who have to label it say?"[17]

ANOTHER LOSS

In March 1997, Blume's close friend Leanne Katz died of cancer. She was sixty-five. She was also the only executive director the National Coalition Against Censorship had ever known in its twenty years of existence. The NCAC was formed in 1974 in response to the Supreme Court ruling in *Miller v. California*, which effectively made it easier to censor and ban books that, according to the written decision, lacked "serious literary, artistic, political, or scientific value."[18]

During her tenure, Katz was known for tirelessly defending dozens of authors, including Maurice Sendak, Robert Cormier, Mark Twain, and of course Judy Blume.

"When my books were being banned early on, in the eighties, I had nowhere to go, until I found this remarkable woman, this tiny dynamo who had such passion and energy for fighting censorship," Blume said in eulogy. "From then on, if I had word from a teacher, a librarian, or a newspaper anywhere in the country that something was being banned, all I had to do was put this person in touch with Leanne, and I knew she would instantly respond and get them through this, let them know they were not alone. She believed in the First Amendment above all."[19]

Blume revealed that Katz had been troubled in her final days because in addition to removing books from schools, the teachers and librarians who chose or recommended them were also being fired. But Judy had a more cautiously optimistic view because she believed people were fighting back. She thinks most Americans stayed uninvolved initially because they really weren't paying attention to what was happening.

"The publishers, the libraries and teachers were caught out because they weren't prepared," she explained. "Now all libraries are told to have policies in place. Parents can't just frighten a teacher or a librarian in the way they used to, when they could come into school waving any old book that they hadn't even read in the first place." Although she recounted stories of teachers being threatened or having their houses firebombed, she still felt "more optimistic now than if you had asked me five years ago."[20]

Optimistic yes, but still aware the battles were far from over. In 1997, the Elgin, Illinois, school district—the second largest in the state—banned *Forever* from its middle school libraries after a handful of parents complained. It was the first time any book had ever been pulled from a middle school in that district.

A spokesperson for the American Library Association in Chicago said, "School libraries are still dealing with children of many ages, who mature at different rates, who have different life experiences, upbringings and family values. We are not all cut from the same cloth. The needs that people have are not identical. Judy Blume's *Forever* might be exactly what some young person needs."[21]

Two years later, an attempt was made to return *Forever* to middle school library shelves and both sides argued before the school board. Librarian Joan Devine defended the book. "I hope to instill in my children a love for reading and books, not a fear of books," she told the board. "At middle-school age, they are not young children anymore. They begin to think about sex and keep their thoughts to themselves a little more."[22]

Another parent spoke angrily against the book—even though her own children were home-schooled and didn't attend any middle school in the district. She claimed the issue was the taxpayers' right to determine standards.

"I was horrified at how far this thing has gone. Parents do not have a say-so," Jean McNamara claimed. "Librarians can choose books, and that is called selection. But when parents want a book removed, it's censorship."[23]

In the end, the board deadlocked in a three-three vote, so *Forever* remained banned. Per local rules, the matter could not be brought before the board again for two years. One school board member, Doug Heaton, said: "As a board, we must decide what is right, not who is right. . . . You may vote to protect pornography, but I vote to protect children."[24]

Fellow board member Karen Carney saw it differently. "Every parent has the right to make decisions for their child, but only for their child. Children need lots of opportunities and need to be exposed to other ways of thinking."[25]

And despite the ongoing challenges, Blume had every intention of giving her readers, both young and old, relevant books to ponder.

NOTES

1. Amy Krouse Rosenthal, "Are You There Judy?" http://www.heebmagazine. com/articles/view/89 (accessed July 13, 2007).

2. Linda Richards, "Interview: Judy Blume," *January Magazine*, 1998, http:// januarymagazine.com/profiles/blume.html.

3. Ibid.

4. Ibid.

5. Julie Salamon, "Young Audience Grows Up," *New York Times*, April 12, 2004.

6. "Margaret A. Edwards Award For Outstanding Literature For Young Adults," listing of awards given1988–present, http://thelibrary.org/teens/bledwd. cfm (accessed July 13, 2007).

7. Teenreads.com, "Author Profile: Judy Blume," http://www.teenreads.com/ authors/au-blume-judy.asp (accessed July 13, 2007).

8. Brooks Whitney, "Judy Blume Gets Real. She Wrote the Book on Growing Pains," *Chicago Tribune*, November 23, 1993, Kidnews, pg. 1.

9. Carol Stocker, "Reading Judy Blume," *Boston Globe*, October 22, 1981, http: //infoweb.newsbank.com/iw-search/we/InfoWeb?p_action=doc&p_ docid=0EB9757462953297&p_docnum=8&p_queryname=2&p_product= NewsBank&p_theme=aggregated4&p_nbid=P5DL52JLMTE4MjExMTQ0 My4yMjgyOTU6MTo4OnJhLTE5NDQ5.

10. Connie G. Rockman, ed., *Eighth Book of Junior Authors and Illustrators* (New York: H. W. Wilson, 2000).

11. Ellen Barry, "Judy Blume for President," *Boston Phoenix*, May 26, 1998, http://weeklywire.com/ww/05–26–98/boston_feature_1.html.

12. Paula Span, "Late Blumers," *Washington Post*, August 24, 1998, http:// www.highbeam.com/doc/1P2–682067.html.

13. Andrew Graham-Dixon, "Nom De Blume," *The Independent*, October 15, 1996, http://www.highbeam.com/doc/1P2–4829518.html.

14. Ibid.

15. Ibid.

16. Ibid.

17. Sandy Rovner, "Judy Blume: Talking It Out," *Washington Post*, November 3, 1981, B1.

18. *Miller v. California*, 413 U.S. 15 (1973).

19. Tamar Lewin, "Leanne Katz, 65, Director Of Anti-Censorship Coalition," *New York Times*, March 5, 1997, B5, http://www.katz.us/LeanneKatz.htm.

20. Ibid.

21. Dimitra DeFotis, "School Ban On Blume Book May End," *Chicago Tribune*, June 14, 1999, Metro, p. 1.

22. Ibid.

23. Ibid.

24. Mary Alice Benoit, "Book By Blume To Stay Banned At Junior Highs," *Chicago Tribune*, June 22, 1999, Metro, p. 2.

25. Ibid.

Chapter 13

SISTERHOOD

Judy Blume's third adult book, *Summer Sisters*, was literally a labor of love. The book took her around three years to write and more than twenty-two drafts to polish. She calls it her book from hell that "was very tough to get right because these two young women were on my mind for a long time."[1]

The germ of the idea for *Summer Sisters* was planted back in 1983. That was the year Judy first visited Martha's Vineyard. Blume admits she had never really heard of the quaint seaside community before. That first summer, they stayed in a house George's daughter Amanda dubbed the Psycho House. But when they came back the next time, they fell in love with the house they rented that year. A few years later they bought the property. And over the next ten years the idea of the story simmered in the back of Judy's brain and the characters slowly took shape.

But the road from that first spark of inspiration to the finished book was long and arduous. "Many times while I was writing it I thought I just couldn't. It was so hard,"[2] she says. However, there was never any real question that she would eventually finish the book. "It haunted me, I had to go back and do it. I couldn't let the characters go, they were so real."[3]

There were times Judy thought she would never finish the book, a complicated tale that intertwines many lives, many relationships, and many years. "I'm very insecure about my writing,"[4] she admits, which explains why she kept an ongoing *Anxiety Diary* on her Web site that chronicled her emotional struggles with *Summer Sisters*—worrying whether it was good enough, if she was making a mistake by writing it at all, if her fans would hate it, if anyone would buy it, if anyone would show up for her scheduled book signings, if it would be the end of her career.

Despite finding this book especially difficult to write, Judy stuck to her usual routine, noting, "Once I begin a new book, the most important part of the process is perseverance." She says. "I try to write seven days a week, if only for an hour or two, until I have a first draft."[5]

Judy says she loves getting inside her characters' heads, because "what we think is not necessarily what we say or do. Discovering those voices is when the book started to come together."[6]

Judy is a morning writer, getting dressed for the day and sitting down at her desk in her home office around 9:00 A.M., as if she were reporting to a regular job—her longtime fantasy. She remembers she once actually rented an outside office. It was right after she and her kids had moved to New Mexico with Tom Kitchens and she was having a hard time getting started with a new book. "I convinced myself that if I left the house each morning with the rest of the family, I would solve my problem." But she had rented a space above a bakery, "and the delicious aroma of freshly baked bread and pastries drove me wild. Every day at noon I would rush downstairs to buy two glazed donuts and by three o'clock I would crave another round. After a few months and a few pounds I moved home again."[7]

During the first draft of a book, which is the hardest time for her, Judy sits determinedly at her desk—"I check my watch a lot and hope the phone will ring—anything to make the time go faster."[8] If she has a good morning writing, she may put in a few more hours after lunch. Otherwise, she calls it a day.

But once the rewriting starts, Blume's work hours are longer and more intense. With each rewrite, she becomes more immersed and less social. When it's finally ready to go to the editor, she suffers an emotional letdown. "I feel sad. It's like having to say good-bye to a close friend. The best therapy is becoming involved with a new project."[9]

After turning in the manuscript to her editor, Blume remembers begging her husband, "You have to help me get this book back. . . . We're going to give back the advance and we're going to stop this book. I've had a wonderful, long career and I don't want to go out this way."

George took her panic in stride and dryly suggested, "Why don't you just leave the country? Come back in a few months and it'll all be over."[10]

Judy says that there are times, like in her most difficult moments writing *Summer Sisters,* that she thinks "I don't want to do this anymore. . . . It's too hard, too painful. But then I think, you don't decide whether to write or not. You just have to do it."[11]

Obviously, *Summer Sisters* was not the literary, personal, or career disaster Blume feared. So when she read it later, it amused her. "Ironically, despite all my fears and setbacks, the book turned out to be my biggest success. I guess the way things turned out, you've learned never to indulge that kind of anxiety again."[12]

That said, Judy has to always remind herself not to let reviews rattle her. "I promise myself I won't become obsessed by reviews," she wrote in her online diary. "I won't read the bad ones more than once. Maybe twice. I'll focus on the good ones—if there are any good ones."[13]

VIX AND CAITLIN

> Everyone in Vix's sixth grade class was so in love with [Caitlin]. But Vix was too shy, too quiet to even speak her name. She sat back and worshiped from afar as the others fought over who would get to be her partner, who would share desks with her. So she thought she'd heard wrong when Caitlin asked, "Want to come away with me this summer?"
>
> —*Summer Sisters*

Summer Sisters, Blume's twenty-first novel, follows the complex friendship between Victoria, or Vix, and Caitlin. Vix is shy and in awe of Caitlin, a smart, beautiful, charismatic force of energy who can be seductively charming and adventuresome one moment, edgy and disgruntled then next. When Caitlin invites Vix to spend the summer with her and her family on Martha's Vineyard, Vix can't believe her good fortune. At the beach, the twelve-year-olds forge a special, intimate bond that leads to some sexual play. They also promise each other they will never be ordinary. Over the next twenty years their lives will take unexpected turns, as will their friendship. "I think it's a friendship more intense and long lasting than many love affairs," Blume says, adding, "Caitlin represents one side of me, and Vix another. I was the good girl but excited by the idea of being the bad girl."[14]

Summer Sisters is dedicated to Mary Weaver, Judy's best friend since seventh grade and the woman she describes as her soul mate. They met in homeroom class and remained inseparable best friends through high school. Judy says they remain friends for life. "Our history runs deep. Our genuine feelings for one another, deeper."[15]

For many years, the two women rarely saw each other but began to spend more time together again in recent years. "We married, had babies, went to work, lost parents. . . . But when we're together the years fall away.

Isn't that what matters? To have someone who can remember with you? To have someone who remembers how far you've come?"[16]

Even though the book is dedicated to Mary Weaver, Judy's best friend since seventh grade, the author denies the book is autobiographical. In fact, she says it probably is the least autobiographical of any of her books. But, she acknowledges, "I allow my characters to live out my fantasies."[17]

However, Blume does admit that the scenes of physical intimacy shared by Vix had a basis in real life. "I played sexual games . . . with one friend. We've never spoken about it. I still know her. She's not my best friend. That period ended very quickly. Of course, I sent her a copy of *Summer Sisters*, but I've never heard from her."[18]

For the first time in many years, Blume did a book tour to promote *Summer Sisters*. She kept a running journal of her travels in the online Anxiety Diary. Judy found it fun to know that "whatever happens to me during the day—good, bad or indifferent—I get to write it down . . . and it's out there. And maybe nobody in the world cares, but I've always found that kind of writing to be cathartic."[19]

> This morning's author escort wants to talk on the way to the airport. The problem with author escorts is they want to be friendly and chat with you and when you don't feel up to it you run the risk of being seen as difficult. So this morning I'm difficult . . ."[20]

The tour was exhausting, the days starting early in the morning and going late into the evening. But the pleasure of meeting women who had grown up reading her books made the effort worth it. "I'm meeting these generations who really are grown up now who grew up on my books. Some of them have kids and they bring their kids and that's exciting. It's fun."[21]

Judy says many women told her she had saved their life as a teenager; some cried. "My success has always come from readers, not from critics," she explains.[22] When asked if she thought there was any difference between young readers today as compared to those thirty years ago, Blume said, "I don't think people change. Everything around us changes, but the human condition doesn't change. What's important to us remains the same, and that's what links everyone together. It's that inside stuff: the need for love and acceptance, and getting to know yourself and your place in the world."[23]

For all of Judy's worries that *Summer Sisters* could ruin her career, it became the best-selling book of her career. And added another chapter to the Blume mystique.

NOTES

1. Ellen Kenner, "Judy Blume," http://www.bookpage.com/9805bp/judy_blume.html (accessed July 13, 2007).

2. Linda Richards, "Interview: Judy Blume," *January Magazine*, 1998http://januarymagazine.com/profiles/blume.html.

3. Teenreads.com, "Author Profile: Judy Blume," http://www.teenreads.com/authors/au-blume-judy.asp (accessed July 13, 2007).

4. M. L. Lyke, "The Grown-Up World of Judy Blume," *Seattle Post-Intelligencer*, May 30, 1998, http://www.highbeam.com/doc/1a1-64588190.html.

5. Judy Blume, "Judy Blume Talks About Writing: A Personal View," ehttp://www.judyblume.com/writing-jb.html#A%20writer's%20lif (accessed July 13, 2007).

6. Ibid.

7. Alison Dorfman, "Alison Dorfman Interviews Judy Blume," http://www.randomhouse.com/boldtype/0698/blume/interview.html (accessed July 13, 2007).

8. Ibid.

9. Ibid.

10. Jennifer Frey, "Fiction Heroine," *Washington Post*, November 17, 2004, C1.

11. Herbert N. Foerstel, *Banned in the U.S.A.: A Reference Guide to Book Censorship in Schools and Public Libraries* (Westport: Greenwood Press, 2002), p. 131.

12. M. L. Lyke, "The Grown-Up World of Judy Blume," *Seattle Post-Intelligencer*, May 30, 1998, http://www.highbeam.com/doc/1a1-64588190.html.

13. Judy Blume, "Judy's Anxiety Diary," http://www.judyblume.com/ss-diary6.html (accessed July 10, 2007).

14. Ellen Kanner, "A Woman for All Seasons Reflects on Growing Up and Growing Older," http://www.bookpage.com/9805bp/judy_blume.html (accessed July 10, 2007).

15. M. L. Lyke, "The Grown-Up World of Judy Blume," *Seattle Post-Intelligencer*, May 30, 1998.

16. Judy Blume, "Best Friends," http://www.randomhouse.com/features/blume/scrapbook.html (accessed July 10, 2007).

17. Ibid.

18. William Leith, "Teen Spirit," *The Independent (London)*, July 18, 1999, http://www.highbeam.com/doc/1P2–5001703.html.

19. Judy Blume, "Best Friends," http://www.randomhouse.com/features/blume/scrapbook.html (accessed July 10, 2007).

20. Agnes Garrett and Helga P. McCue, *Authors and Artists for Young Adults*, vol. 3 (Farmington Hills, Mich.: Thomson Gale), pp. 25–36.

21. Judy Blume, "Judy's Anxiety Diary," http://www.judyblume.com/ss-diary6.html (accessed July 10, 2007).

22. M. L. Lyke, "The Grown-Up World of Judy Blume," *Seattle Post-Intelligencer*, May 30, 1998.

23. Alison Dorfman, "Alison Dorfman Interviews Judy Blume," http://www.randomhouse.com/boldtype/0698/blume/interview.html (accessed July 10, 2007).

Chapter 14

STILL IN THE LIMELIGHT

The life of a writer is, if nothing else, always an adventure. Even for an established writer like Judy Blume, nothing is a given—including getting a book published. After she finished *Summer Sisters*, she sent it off to a couple of her longtime publishers—who stunned her by rejecting the book. They couldn't decide whether it was a novel for adults or young adults, so they passed. It wounded Blume to her core.

"They didn't have faith in me, didn't think that I could revise it. It was very painful. You know, you don't expect rejection at this point in your career. Especially since *Wifey* and *Smart Women*—my first two novels for adults—were bestsellers." She ran into a novelist she knew, and after literally crying on his shoulder, he told her not to give up. "Don't give in, it's going to work,"[1] she remembers him saying. She took his advice and ended up with the biggest success of her career.

The upside of writing is that the world is your canvass—you never know where you will find inspiration. Judy remembers the day she was out kayaking when she heard a loud, somewhat scary noise that sounded like gunfire. She looked toward the shore and saw a group of people running down a hill . . . dressed in formal clothes. "Then I could make out that there was a bride and groom. They, along with everyone else, jumped into the pond. When I realized it was a celebration, I said to myself, *I'm going to start [Summer Sisters] at a wedding.* I came back and wrote the wedding scene immediately, just as I saw it."[2]

Sometimes, inspiration comes from pain and loss. In 1999, Judy edited a collection of previously unpublished stories by censored authors. The collection was called *Places I Never Meant to Be*. The story behind the book is one that can still make Blume cry. Her dear friend, Leanne Katz, was gravely ill. It was clear she was dying, so a group of her friends and associates wanted to do something to honor her and her life's work.

"David Gale at Simon and Schuster suggested that I edit a collection of original pieces by banned authors," Judy recalls, saying the idea appealed to her a lot. "It would be a way to raise some much needed funds for NCAC and it would also serve as a tribute to Leanne.

"I talked to Leanne just two days before her death. She knew she was dying, yet she was fund-raising to the end. She said, *Use me, tell everybody, write letters, do whatever you can to keep NCAC going*. She never lost her sense of humor. I spoke at her memorial service, but I'm so hopelessly emotional that I had difficulty maintaining my composure."[3]

The book gave Judy a pulpit to challenge those who would try to impose their beliefs on others by taking away their freedom to pursue ideas found in books. "If those of us who care about making our own decisions about what to read and what to think don't take a stand, others will decide for us. I've never been one to let others decide what's right for me or my children," Blume says.[4]

In the introduction to *Places I Never Meant to Be*, Blume writes impassionedly about the need for writers to create without fear. In this environment on ongoing attempts to censor ideas and written words, Judy says, "I mourn the loss of books that will never be written, I mourn the voices that will be silenced—writers' voices, teachers' voices, students' voices—and all because of fear. How many have resorted to self-censorship? How many are saying to themselves, *Nope . . . can't write about that. Can't teach that book. Can't have that book in our collection. Can't let my student write that editorial in the school paper . . .*"[5]

She also worries about the loss young people will suffer. "Instead of finding the novels that illuminate life, they will find only those materials to which nobody could possibly object."[6]

All the royalties from *Places I Never Meant to Be* were donated to the NCAC in honor of Katz. Judy encouraged young writers to follow their hearts and to be unafraid. "Write honestly. Write from deep inside. Leanne used to say, *It's your job to write as well as you can, Judy. It's my job to defend what you've written*. But Leanne couldn't do it on her own. No one can. It's up to all of us."[7]

FUDGE REDUX

Sometimes inspiration comes from the most everyday event. One day, Judy and her grandson Elliot were having a pancake breakfast at Ricky's

Blue Heaven in Key West. A local artisan was there selling bracelets and Elliot wanted his grandmother to buy one. Judy tried to divert his interest by saying she didn't have any more money. He looked at her and said, "Just go to the cash machine."

"That was the *Ah, ha!* moment," she says.[8] "Kids think money comes from the ATM. The concept of money is hard for them."[9] And just like that, Judy found herself revisiting the Hatchers. "At the end of writing every book I think, I'm never doing this again! But when it's published and I sniff the pages—something I did as a preschooler at the public library—I'm awfully glad I did! And if the bug bites . . ."[10]

Judy began writing the book in Key West during 2001. Three of the chapters were going to be based on a real-life trip she had taken with Elliot to Washington, D.C., including a tour they took of the FBI. And then the terrorist attack on September 11, 2001, happened. "Suddenly those chapters weren't funny," Blume says somberly.[11]

She relates an eerie incident. When they visited the FBI, they got a copy of the Most Wanted List. Listed as number one was someone they had never yet heard of: Osama Bin Laden. So back home, she had written a scene where Fudge sees the $5 million reward offered for Bin Laden and announces he's going to find him so he can be rich. Obviously, there was no way Blume could leave that scene in.

The attacks affected her so deeply, Blume wasn't sure she'd ever be able to finish the book. "I thought, *Who cares?* and *What does this matter?* It was a very gloomy time."[12]

But she eventually went back to the book after George rented her a room at a local inn. Judy would ride her bike over every morning, and in the quiet solitude, began writing again. "It was the most spontaneous writing I had done in a while."[13]

In *Double Fudge*, the fifth book to feature the irrepressible younger Hatcher brother, Fudge is obsessed with money. He even creates his own currency called Fudge Bucks. But over the course of the book, he slowly learns that the most important things in life can't be bought. Although it had been twelve years since *Fudge-a-Mania*, Blume says, "It felt as if I'd never been away from them at all."[14]

Once again, Judy found herself on a book tour, which included speaking engagements at schools, where she presented a slide show titled "My Life as a Writer" that was both a professional and personal retrospective. Although she thought *Summer Sisters* was going to be her last book tour, Judy gets a special joy interacting in person with her youngest fans. She also feels a special responsibility when writing for younger readers, "to tell the most honest stories I can." And she always feels it's her responsibility "to tell the best story I can, to work until it feels as right as I can get it," whether writing for younger readers or for an adult audience. "The process is the same," she says. "I just have to get inside the heads of different age groups. I like to deal with the side of me that's a grown woman from time to time, anyway."[15]

In March, 2004, Walt Disney Pictures announced plans to develop and produce films based on Judy Blume books, beginning with *Deenie*. Nina Jacobson, then-president of the Buena Vista Motion Pictures Group, said in the press announcement: "The name Judy Blume is synonymous with great young adult literature. Everyone discovers her books in fifth grade and grows up with her. She strikes a chord with humor and heart while never preaching."[16]

Larry Blume, who would produce the film, commented, "Anyone who is my age or younger grew up with Judy Blume books, so the movie industry is just coming to understand who she is. In the publishing world everyone knows how popular she is," he said, "but in movies and television in a strange way she's—not quite a secret—but they had no idea how many books she's sold."[17]

The deal came about after Disney executive Karen Glass discovered a producer she knew who shared an office space with Judy. Glass had grown up reading Blume and immediately put her connection to use.

Judy says that over the years there had been a lot of conversations about making more movies based on her books, but nothing ever came from it. So she was extremely enthusiastic to hook up with Disney and to work again with her son Larry. "We've all waited a long time for this moment and are excited by the possibilities," she said. "Can't wait to get going!"[18]

Later that year, the National Book Foundation honored Blume with its Medal for Distinguished Contribution to American Letters—the first time a young adult novelist had ever received the award. The enormity of the honor initially escaped her. She admits she had to look the award up to see what it was. Then she was humbled.

"For me, it's a huge honor—and I think for all of us who write for children and encourage kids to read through our books because I don't consider this just for me. I think it is a way to honor children's books."[19]

The ceremony was held in November 2004 at the Marriott Marquis Hotel in New York. In an emotional speech in front of her peers, colleagues, friends, and families, Judy spoke of the importance of writing in her life, her fervent belief that censorship has no place in America, and her gratitude at those who took her books to heart.

I have my readers to thank for my career and not a day goes by that I don't remember that. I doubt there's a more loyal, supportive audience anywhere and almost from the start, as many of you know, they have written to me. So I wanted to share a couple of their earliest letters, which remain my favorites.

"Dear Judy, My mom never talks to me about the things young girls think most about. She doesn't know how I feel. I don't know where I stand in the world. I don't know who I am. That's why I read. To find myself."

And Elizabeth, wherever you are, you are the reason I continue to write.[20]

REFLECTION

At the end of her presentation and slide show for school students Judy always says, "I'm really happy being me."[21]

Professionally speaking, she has good reason to be. Her books and novels have sold more than seventy-five million copies and have been translated into at least twenty languages. She has won dozens of awards and citations, changed the way publishers and readers alike view young adult literature, and raised awareness on the importance of maintaining a free environment for writers to pursue their craft.

"The funny thing about writing is you don't decide to do it," Blume muses. "You wouldn't do it if you didn't have to. I always say, *This is it. I'm never going through this again.* But after a while I do. . . . It's inside me. I have no choice." Blume says she is blessed to find inspiration in her readers. "I am surely the luckiest writer in the world to have such a close connection to my readers," whom she thanks for giving their support and encouragement over the years. "My husband, George, says whenever I feel down and wonder what I'm doing, all I have to do is read my e-mail."[22]

Aware that there is more life behind her than in front of her, Judy admits, "These days I stop and think before I start a new book and ask myself do I really want to spend the next year or two or three with these characters because if I don't, then I shouldn't be writing about them. I think as you grow older you realize you only have time for so many more books.[23]

"I'm much more anxious now than in the beginning, when I knew nothing, when I had no fears about submitting anything, and I wrote book after book after book for a very long time. I think success makes you more fearful," she says.[24]

"But no, I have no regrets. I just have lots of ideas![25] I hope I get to write all of them."[26]

NOTES

1. Amy Krouse Rosenthal, "Are You There Judy?" *HEEB Mag*, 13, http://www.heebmagazine.com/articles/view/89.

2. Ibid.

3. Herbert N. Foerstel, *Banned in the U.S.A.: A Reference Guide to Book Censorship in Schools and Public Libraries* (Westport: Greenwood Press, 2002), p. 132.

4. "Judy Blume: Uncensored," *CNN.com Book News*, August 26, 1999, http://www.cnn.com/books/news/9908/26/blume/index.html.

5. Judy Blume, ed., *Places I Never Meant To Be* (New York: Simon And Shuster, 1999).

6. Ibid.

7. Ibid.

8. Sue Corbett, "Judy Blume Tackles Kids and Money in Her Hero's Latest Adventures," *Miami Herald*, January 15, 2003, http://www.highbeam.com/doc/1G1–119242588.html.

9. Judy Green, "Sense And Censorship," *Sacramento Bee*, October 2, 2002, Scene E1.

10. Karen MacPherson, "A Fourth Helping of 'Fudge,'" *Washington Post*, December 16, 2002, C14.

11. Herbert N. Foerstel, *Banned in the U.S.A.: A Reference Guide to Book Censorship in Schools and Public Libraries*, (Westport: Greenwood Press, 2002), p. 140.

12. Sue Corbett, "Judy Blume Tackles Kids and Money in Her Hero's Latest Adventures," *Miami Herald*, January 15, 2003, http://www.highbeam.com/doc/1G1–119242588.html.

13. Ibid.

14. Carolyn Mackler, "The Return of Fudge," *Parenting*, September 1, 2002, p. 32.

15. Judy Blume, "Are You There, Reader? It's Me, Judy," *Chicago Sun-Times*, July 5, 1998, http://www.highbeam.com/doc/1P2–4455974.html.

16. Press release.

17. United Press International, "Hollywood Finally Discovers Judy Blume," April 8, 2004.

18. Press release.

19. Michelle Norris, "Interview: Judy Blume Discusses Her Career as a Successful and Controversial Author of Books for Young Readers," NPR: *All Things Considered*, September 15, 2004, http://www.highbeam.com/doc/1P1–107433907.html.

20. National Book Awards, Judy Blume to Receive the Medal for Distinguished Contribution to American Letters from the National Book Foundation, September 15, 2004, http://www.nationalbook.org/dcal_2004_pr.html.

21. Jessica Mosby, University Wire, October 7, 2002.

22. Judy Blume, "Are You There, Reader? It's Me, Judy," *Chicago Sun-Times*, July 5, 1998, http://www.highbeam.com/doc/1P2-4455974.html.

23. Ibid.

24. Simon Houpt, "Blume's Last Words?" *Globe & Mail*, November 30, 2002, http://www.theglobeandmail.com/servlet/story/LAC.20021130.BKJUDY/PPVStory?URL_Article_ID=LAC.20021130.BKJUDY&DENIED=1.

25. "Author Chat with Judy Blume," *TeenLink*, New York Public Library Web site, November 19, 2002, http://teenlink.nypl.org/blume_txt.html.

26. "Author Profile: Judy Blume," Teenreads.com, 2003, http://www.teenreads.com/authors/au-blume-judy.asp.

BIBLIOGRAPHY

Anderson, John T. "Conjuring Controversy Potter Books Provoke Powerful Opinions About Freedom Of Speech." *The Times Record*, April 27, 2003, http://swtimes.com/articles/2003/04/27/insight/export63388.txt.

———. "Harry Potter to Appear on Shelves." *The Times Record*, April 23, 2003, http://swtimes.com/articles/2003/04/23/news/export63254.txt.

———. "'Potter' Pickle Pricey." *The Times Record*, April 25, 2003, http://swtimes.com/articles/2003/04/25/news/export63334.txt.

Anderson, Kathryn. "No Blume Fan." *Chicago Tribune*, March 30, 1985, Perspective, 8.

Are You There Judy? http://www.heebmagazine.com/articles/view/89.

"Ask Them Yourself." *Family Weekly*, http://www.newspaperarchive.com/Pdf Viewer.aspx?img=47394592.

Author Chat with Judy Blume, November 19th, 2002, http://teenlink.nypl.org/blume_txt.html.

Authors: Judy Blume, Random House, http://www.randomhouse.com/author/results.pperl?authorid=2611&view=full_sptlght.

Authors and Artists for Young Adults on Judy Blume. BookRrags.com, http://www.bookrags.com/biography/judy-blume-aya/.

Barry, Ellen. "Judy Blume for President." *The Boston Phoenix*, May 26, 1998, http://weeklywire.com/ww/05-26-98/boston_feature_1.html.

Benoit, Mary Alice. "Book By Blume To Stay Banned At Junior Highs." *Chicago Tribune*. June 22, 1999. Metro Northwest, 2.

Blume, Judy. *Are You There God? It's Me, Margaret*. Englewood Cliffs, N.J.: Bradbury Press, 1970 (Paperback Dell).

———. "Are you there, reader? It's me, Judy." *Chicago Sun-Times*. July 5, 1998.

————. *Blubber*. Scarsdale, N.Y.: Bradbury Press, 1974. (Paperback Dell) http://www.judyblume.com/blubber.html.

————. "Dear Judy, Letters Address Children's Secret Feelings." *Chicago Tribune*. May 4, 1986, Tempo, 1.

————. *Deenie*. Scarsdale, N.Y.: Bradbury Press, 1973. (Paperback Dell).

————. *Double Fudge*. New York: Dutton Children's Books, 2002. (Paperback Penguin).

————. *Freckle Juice*. New York: Four Winds Press, 1971. (Paperback Dell).

————. *Forever*. Scarsdale, N.Y.: Bradbury Press, 1975. (Paperback Dell) http://www.judyblume.com/forever.html.

————. *Fudge-A-Mania*. New York: Dutton, 1990 (Paperback Dell) http://www.judyblume.com/fudge-a-mania.html.

————. "Helping Kids Deal With Divorce." *The San Francisco Chronicle*, May 1, 1986. People, 27.

————. *Here's To You, Rachel Robinson*. New York: Orchard Books, 1993. (Paperback Dell).

————. *Iggie's House*. Englewood Cliffs, N.J.: Bradbury Press, 1970. (Paperback Dell).

————. Interview by Michelle Norris. Tape recording. September 15. National Public Radio, All Things Considered, 2004.

————. "Is Harry Potter Evil?" *New York Times*. October 22, 1999.

————. *It's Not The End Of The World*. Scarsdale, N.Y.: Bradbury Press, 1972. (Paperback Dell).

————. *The Judy Blume Diary*. New York: Yearling, 1981.

————. *Just As Long As We're Together*. New York: Orchard Books, 1987. (Paperback Dell) http://www.judyblume.com/just-as.html.

————. *Letters To Judy: What Kids Wish They Could Tell You*. New York: G.P. Putnam's Sons, 1986. (Paperback Pocket Books).

————. *The One In The Middle Is The Green Kangaroo*. Chicago, Reilly & Lee Books, 1969. (Paperback Dell).

————. *Otherwise Known As Sheila The Great*. New York: Dutton, 1972. (Paperback Dell) http://www.judyblume.com/sheila.html.

————. *The Pain And The Great One*. Scarsdale, N.Y.: Bradbury Press, 1984. (Paperback Dell) http://www.judyblume.com/pain.html.

————. Personal Message, February, 2004, at http://www.judyblume.com.

————, ed. *Places I Never Meant To Be*. New York: Simon and Schuster for Young Readers, 1999.

————. "She Still Knows You Best: Judy Blume Scrapbook," *Best Friends*, http://www.randomhouse.com/features/blume/scrapbook.html.

————. *Smart Women*. New York: Putnam, 1983. (Paperback Pocket Books).

———. *Starring Sally J. Freedman As Herself*. Scarsdale, N.Y.: Bradbury Press, 1977. (Paperback Dell).

———. *Summer Sisters*. New York: Delacorte Press, 1998. (Paperback Dell).

———. *Superfudge*. New York: Dutton, 1980. (Paperback Dell).

———. *Tales Of A Fourth Grade Nothing*. New York: Dutton, 1972. (Paperback Dell).

———. *Then Again, Maybe I Won't*. Scarsdale, N.Y.: Bradbury Press, 1971. (Paperback Dell)

———. *Tiger Eyes*. Scarsdale, N.Y.: Bradbury Press, 1981. (Paperback Dell).

———. *Wifey*. New York: Putnam, 1978. (Paperback Pocket Books).

Bryant, Amy. *Talks with Judy Blume*, teenwire.com. May 22, 2007, http://www.teenwire.com/infocus/2007/if-20070522p487-blume.php (Used with Permission from Planned Parenthood Federation of America, Inc.)

"Censors Busy In the Schools." *The San Francisco Chronicle*, August 16, 1985, pg. 49.

Chevalier, Tracy (ed.). *Twentieth Century Children Writers*; St. James Press: New York, 1989.

CNN. Books—Judy Blume: Uncensored—August 26, 1999, http://www.cnn.com/books/news/9908/26/blume/index.html.

Coburn, Randy Sue. "A Best-Selling But Much-Censored Author." *San Francisco Chronicle*. August 12, 1985, 15.

Corbett, Sue. "Judy Blume Tackles Kids and Money in her Hero's Latest Adventures." *The Miami Herald*, January 15, 2003.

Counts v. Cedarville School District, No. 02-2155 (W.D. Ark. April 22, 2003)

Counts v. Cedarville School District Decision, http://www.arwd.uscourts.gov/go/files/02-2155-mo-wp.

DeFotis, Dimitra. "School Ban On Blume Book May End." *Chicago Tribune*. June 14, 1999. Northwest, 1.

Dictionary of Literary Biography on Judy (Sussman) Blume, http://www.bookrags.com/biography/judy-sussman-blume-dlb/.

Eighth Book of Junior Authors and Illustrators. H. W. Wilson Company. 2000.

"8 Who Write Children's Books Protest Ban on Blume Works." November 20, 1984, http://query.nytimes.com/gst/fullpage.html?res=9904E6D91F39F933A15752C1A962948260.

Encyclopedia of World Biography on Judy Blume, http://www.bookrags.com/biography/judy-blume/.

"Federal court foils Arkansas school's effort to restrict Harry Potter." *Church & State*, June 2003, http://findarticles.com/p/articles/mi_qa3944/is_200306/ai_n9283016.

Feinberg, Lawrence. "Schools' Use Of Candid Novels Draws Parents' Fire." *Washington Post*, February 25, 1980, A1.

Felsenthal, Carol. "Judy Blume Grows Up." American Library Assn.

Flaste, Richard. "Viewing childhood as it is." *New York Times*. September 29, 1976.

Foerstel, Herbert N. *Banned in the U.S.A.: A Reference Guide to Book Censorship in Schools and Public Libraries*. Westport, CT: Greenwood Press. 2002.

Freeman, Judy. "Talking with Judy Blume." *Instructor*. May 1, 2005, http://www.highbeam.com/doc/1G1-132531055.html.

Frey, Jennifer. "Fiction Heroine." *Washington Post*. November 17, 2004.

Garrett, Agnes and Helga P. McCue. *Authors and Artists for Young Adults*, v. 3, Farmington Hills, MI: Thomson Gale.

Goldblatt, Jennifer. "Blume's Day." *The New York Times*. November 14, 2004, 1.

Gorner, Peter. "The Giddy/Sad, Flighty/Solid Life Of Judy Blume." *Chicago Tribune*. March 15, 1985.

Graham-Dixon, Andrew. "Nom De Blume." *The Independent*. October 15, 1996.

Green, Judy. "Sense and Censorship." *The Sacramento Bee*. October 2, 2002, E1.

Green, Michelle. *People Weekly*; March 19, 1984.

Grossman, Mary. "Blume Doesn't Sound Too Convincing When She Talks About Retiring." *Knight Ridder/Tribune News Service*. October 9, 2002.

Herbert, Rosemary. "A Kid At Heart; Children's Author Judy Blume Brings Back Antics Of Fudge." *The Boston Herald*. October 18, 2002.

"Hollywood finally discovers Judy Blume." United Press International, April 8, 2004.

I Love Email. August—September 2002, http://www.cynthialeitichsmith.com/auth-illJudyBlume.html.

Interview with Judy Blume, Random House.com, http://www.randomhouse.com/teachers/catalog/display.pperl?isbn=9780440407072&view=rg.

Ingram Library Services, *Ingram Explores: Summer Reading*.

Johnson, Wayne. "Blume Book Is Adapted For Seattle Stage." *The Seattle Times*. March 13, 1987. Tempo, 14.

Judy Blume by David Rees. BookRags.com, http://www.bookrags.com/criticism/blume-judy-sussman-kitchens-1938_2/.

Judy Blume Goes Hollywood (Finally.) Plastic, http://www.plastic.com/article.html; sid=04/04/09/14122366.

"Judy Blume Looks Back." *People*. November 29, 2004, 59.

Judy Blume Official Website Welcome, http://www.judyblume.com/message.html.

Judy's Anxiety Diary, http://www.judyblume.com/ss-diary6.html.

Kahn, Joseph P. "Judy Blume's Summer Camp." *Boston Globe*. July 6, 1995 Living, 61.

Kanner, Ellen. *Judy Blume*, http://www.bookpage.com/9805bp/judy_blume.html.

Kanter, Ellen. "Helping Kids Deal with Divorce." *The San Francisco Chronicle.* May 1, 1986.

Kenney, Michael. "Air Apparent Randy Blume Talks about Her Love of Flying, Her First Novel, and Her Mother, Judy, Who Prefers Land." *Boston Globe*, May 25, 1999, E1.

KidsRead.com. Judy Blume, http://www.kidsreads.com/authors/au-blume-judy. asp.

King, Marsha. "Writing Wrongs." *The Seattle Times*, March 16, 1987, C1.

Klein, Norma. "Some Thoughts on Censorship: An Author Symposium." *Top of the News*, Winter, 1983; EJ276815.

Landsberg, Michele. *Reading for the Love of It*. New York: Prentice Hall Press, 1987.

Lee, Betsy. *Judy Blume's Story*. Minneapolis: Dillon Press. 1977.

Leith, William . "Teen Spirit." *The Independent-London*. July 18, 1999.

Lent, ReLeah and Gloria Pipkin. "We Keep Pedaling." The ALAN Review, 28(2), (2001) 9.

Lewin, Tamar. "Leanne Katz, 65, Director Of Anti-Censorship Coalition." March 5, 1997, http://www.katz.us/LeanneKatz.htm.

Lion and the Unicorn. v. 2, no. 2 (Fall 1978).

Lipsyke, Robert. "A Bridge of Words." *The Nation*. November 21, 1981.

Lyke, M. L. "The Grown-Up World of Judy Blume." *Seattle Post-Intelligencer*. May 30, 1998.

Mackler, Carolyn. "The Return of Fudge." *Parenting*. September 1, 2002, 32.

MacPherson, Karen. "A Fourth Helping of 'Fudge.'" *Washington Post*. December 16, 2002, C14.

Major Authors and Illustrators for Children and Young Adults, 2nd ed., 8 vols. (Gale Group, Farmington Hills, MI: Thomson Gale), 2002.

Margaret A. Edwards Award For Outstanding Literature For Young Adults, http://thelibrary.org/teens/bledwd.cfm.

Maynard, Joyce. "Coming of Age with Judy Blume." *The New York Times*. December 3, 1978.

Mazzarella, Sharon R. and Norma Odom Pecora. *Growing Up Girls: Popular Culture and the Construction of Identity*. New York: Peter Lang, (74) 1999, 46.

McDonald, Matt. "Library Cherishes Far-Flung Pen Pals." *Globe West*. May 4, 2003, 14.

McNulty, Faith. "Children's Books for Christmas," *The New Yorker*, December 5, 1983, 208.

Meet the Writers. Barnes&Nobel.com, http://www.barnesandnoble.com/writers/writerdetails.asp?cid=883118.

Michelson, Herbert A. "Kids Tell Her Their Secrets." *The Sacramento Bee*. May 5, 1986, B03

MSNBC.com. Literary Lightning Rod, *Newsweek*, http://www.msnbc.msn.com/ id/18725395/site/newsweek.

Murphy, Caryle. "Merchandisers Challenge Book Display Ban." *The Washington Post*. July 17, 1985, B8.

Murphy, Caryle. "Judge Bars Book Law Enforcement." *The Washington Post*. July 20, 1985, C1.

National Book Awards Ceremony and Dinner, November 17, 2004, New York Marriott Marquis, NY, New York, http://www.nationalbook.org/dcal_2004_pr.html.

National Coalition Against Censorship, http://www.ncac.org/about/about.cfm.

National Review Online, Books on NRO Weekend: Early Blumers, Kathryn Jean Lopez, http://www.nationalreview.com/weekend/books/books-lopez093000.shtml.

Nemy, Enid. "It's Judy Blume, New Yorker." *New York Times*. October 3,

New York Public Library (online), *Author Chat with Judy Blume*, November 19, 2002, http://teenlink.nypl.org/blume_txt.html.

O'Grady, Kathleen and Paula Wansbrough, *Sweet Secrets: Stories of Menstruation*, Toronto, ON: Second Story Press, 1997.

Oppenheimer, Mark. "Why Judy Blume Endures." *New York Times Book Review*, November 16, 1997.

"Put Harry Potter Back on Shelves, Group Asks." *AP Press Release*, March 4, 2003.

Richards, Linda. "Judy Blume: On Censorship, Enjoying Life, and Staying in the Spotlight for 25 years." *January Magazine*, 1998, http://januarymagazine.com/profiles/blume.html.

Roberts, Cynthia. "Judy Blume: No More Kids' Stuff." *Chronicle-Telegram*. October 20, 1978.

Rogers, Amanda. "Nine Reasons To Scoop Up Judy Blume's Tales Of Fudge Hatcher." *Fort Worth Star-Telegram*. February 11, 2003.

Rousseau, Caryn. "Judge Orders Harry Potter Back onto Shelves." *Associated Press*, April 22, 2003.

Rosenthal, Amy Krouse. "Are You There Judy?" http://www.heebmagazine.com/ articles/view/89.

Rovner, Sandy. "Judy Blume: Talking It Out." *Washington Post*, November 3, 1981, B1.

Salamon, Julie. "Girls' pal breaks into the movies." *International Herald Tribune*. April 10, 2004.

Salamon, Julie. "Young audience grows up." *New York Times*. April 12, 2004.

Shulins, Nancy. "Despite controversy, Judy Blume gaining Fans." *AP Newsfeatures*. March 31 1985.

Span, Paula. "Late Blumers." *The Washington Post*, August 24, 1998.

Stocker, Carol. "Reading Judy Blume." *Boston Globe*. October 22, 1981.

Talk of the Nation: Teens Across America, NPR.org, October 21, 1998, http://www.npr.org/templates/story/story.php?storyId=1009881.

Teenreads.com, Author Profile: Judy Blume, http://www.teenreads.com/authors/au-blume-judy.asp.

Teens@Random.com, Deenie, http://www.randomhouse.com/teens/catalog/display.pperl?isbn=9780440932598.

Telford, Cee. *Judy Blume*. (New York: Rosen Publishing, 2004).

"This Cultural Life." *The Independent on Sunday*. May 29, 2005.

Traister, Rebecca. "Modernizing Margaret." *Chicago Sun-Times*, March 8, 2006.

Trueheart. Charles. "Booksellers & The Battle Joined Anti-Censorship Foundation Formed." *The Washington Post*. June 5, 1990, C1.

The Unites States Constitution Online, http://www.usconstitution.net/const.html.

U-Wire.com. Jessica Mosby, October 7, 2002, http://www.highbeam.com/doc/1P1-68543379.html.

Vesey, Tom. "Banned Books On Display at County Libraries." *The Washington Post*, September 9, 1983, B1.

Walsh, Rebecca Ascher. "The Fudge Report." *Entertainment Weekly* October 11, 2002, 77.

What Do Harry Potter, Captain Underpants and Huck Finn Have in Common?, Center for Individual Freedom, http://www.cfif.org/htdocs/legal_issues/legal_updates/first_amendment_cases/harry_potter_censorship.htm.

"What's Up." www.judyblume.com, February 2004.

Whitney, Brooks. "Judy Blume Gets Real. She Wrote the Book on Growing Pains." *Chicago Tribune*. November 23, 1993.

Writing Life, The, http://www.judyblume.com/writing-jb.html#A%20writer's%20life.

"Why We Like Harry Potter: The Series is a *Book of Virtues* With a Preadolescent Funnybone," Editorial, *Christianity Today*, January 10, 2000, http://www.ctlibrary.com/2577.

INDEX

About the Author

KATHLEEN TRACY is a Los Angeles-based journalist. She is the author of over twenty titles, including *Elvis Presley: A Biography* (2006).